How to
Survive
&
Market
Yourself
in
Management

ANDREW PLENINGER

How to Survive & Market Yourself in Management

57625

amacom
A Division of
American Management Associations

Library of Congress Cataloging in Publication Data

Pleninger, Andrew.
　How to survive & market yourself in management.

　1. Executive ability.　2. Applications for positions.
3. Executives — Recruiting.　　I. Title.
HF5500.2.P53　　650′.14　　77-1409
ISBN 0-8144-5436-4

Third printing

Preface

This book deals with reality. It addresses itself to such matters as subjectivity and objectivity in the business structure. In keeping with this time-saving, objective approach, this book uses the masculine gender — he, him, man, and guy. This is done not out of male chauvinism, but to facilitate writing flow and reading ease. Unfailing use of words like "person" or expressions like "he or she" when referring to a given manager would appear awkward and contrived. The author is aware of, and welcomes, the ever-growing number of women and minorities attaining management status. The subject matter of this book covers problems that are generic and asexual in nature. It relates to the managerial function and mission, not to the sex or race of the manager. Utilization of this book's precepts will help anyone in, or aspiring to, management, regardless of physiological differences. The content transcends the physical and relates to the cerebral.

v

But some caveats for minorities are indicated, if only because many persons in such groups have become conditioned to expect special treatment and accelerated upward mobility as their just due for earlier withholdings, neglect, and career impedances. This approach is one of high subjectivity and disregard for reality.

The author is certainly not a Don Quixote tilting at windmills. Nor is he a martyr, a crusader, or even a reformer, attempting to make sweeping changes to correct past injustices. It is unrealistic as well as a waste of time and effort to hope to radically alter the world, the billions of people in it, and their subjective perceptions and self-oriented values. Jesus tried it without conspicuous success, so who is currently qualified to venture a replay effort? Certainly not the author.

What is being attempted is what is realistically feasible, namely, some self-modification effort by the readers of this book, regardless of age, sex, color, or creed. Suppose a reader is a hot-tempered person who can be counted on to blow his or her top ten times out of ten in similar sets of circumstances. If the author can persuade that reader to proceed objectively by disciplining himself or herself to count to ten before erupting, he or she might explode only five times out of ten. In the eyes of the viewers, such a person would be behaving in a new way, and their reaction to the new behavior would also change. The counterreaction would differ too, and soon it would be a new and better ball game for everyone. Although the hot-tempered reader would not have undergone basic changes through the author's suggestion to behave objectively, his behavior would have improved. This is about the most any of us can ever realistically hope for in our attempt to change established systems and values. All we can ever hope to influence, control, and modify is ourselves as individuals. Since this is at least a hopeful and helpful beginning, let us try it.

This book attempts to stick pins in impossible dreams, and to bring approaches to problems down to levels of possible attainment and effectiveness. We hope to take unreachable subjective fantasies and bring them to realizable levels of objectivity and accomplishment.

Andrew Pleninger

Contents

PART I

How to Survive in Management

All the world's problems stem from excessive subjectivity. Subjectivity is responsible for the narrow, parochial views of self-interest that conflict with equally subjective self-concerns of other people. From our neurologies, physiologies, and psychologies arises the universal individual imperative — "Me first."

This section is devoted to an operational definition of objectivity in the business environment. Numerous examples of the use of this approach are given for effective communication and interpersonal skills.

Objectivity

SUBJECTIVITY VERSUS OBJECTIVITY

Management is popularly thought to be a level reached in the business structure as a reward for superior technological competence. This concept is an extension of the Horatio Alger myth so prevalently believed by American males. Supposedly, the man who makes widgets best will be recognized and promoted until ultimately he becomes president of the widget-making company. Disregarded is the fact that the skills required to make good widgets have nothing to do with those needed to be a successful company president.

Improbable dreams have a limited escapist value. When delusion becomes a substitute for reality, the fantasizer is in trouble. This book addresses itself to dispelling this myth and substituting and spelling out the realities of business life at the management level — what it's like, what the do's and don'ts are, what kind of behavior is expected — in short, how to survive and prosper in management.

The frequently described and decried shortage of management talent in the business world is accurate but highly unspecific. There is no shortage of bodies. There is no lack of intelligent, educated, experienced people. What is wanting is the right attitude and approach to management. In other words, most managers go about their duties in subjective, rather than objective, fashion. They are thus foredoomed to poor and limited performance.

The reader is invited to look up the words subjective, subjectivity, objective, and objectivity in any dictionary for full definitions. Our versions are business-oriented simplifications. A subjective person is self-centered and internally oriented toward his or her personal wants, needs, conveniences, and individuality. Such a person is more responsive to introspection, moods, and what goes on in his or her mind than to what is happening in the external world. An objective person is oriented to external happenings and realities as opposed to internal ideas and concepts that may not relate to actuality or its requirements.

Subjectivity and objectivity are opposites, and are present in combination in all of us to varying degrees. The greater the subjectivity, the less objectivity. Too high a degree of subjectivity interferes with managerial skills. The ingredients most needed for success in management are a high degree of objectivity and a corresponding sublimation of subjectivity. Happily for our purposes, objectivity is not something we are born with or without. Once its ingredients are understood, it can be acquired.

COMPONENTS OF OBJECTIVITY

Neutrality of Approach

An objective manager will approach all his problems with an open, neutral mind. He will not let prejudice, bias, position, or personal experience interfere with an impartial, impersonal diagnosis. Only after he has made an objective analysis will he draw on his experience to prescribe and administer the therapy needed to correct the situation. An objective manager performs as a humanoid computer in his assessments of problem situations. True, the computer can be somewhat influenced by the subjectivity of its analysts and programmers — "garbage in, garbage out" — but its output is pure in that it does not dilute, change, influence, or add to that output. It is completely neutral, and does not add other dimensions to the process.

But we don't have to use the sophisticated computer for our analogy. A simple adding machine will do. No matter how accurately we may punch a series of numbers into it, we're going to come up with a lot of wrong answers if we don't clear the machine first. Leftover numbers from earlier computations will intrude and warp the result. So, as managers, we must clear our mental adding machines before addressing ourselves to finding correct answers to our managerial problems. Leftovers, such as position, prejudice, bias, and prior experience, must be eliminated from the equation so that an accurate, impartial diagnosis of the situation may be made before attempting to arrive at an answer.

We are all governed by two natural laws. The first of these is survival of the fittest. However, in our current society this has been repealed in a manner of speaking. Our do-good, welfare orientation means everyone in the tribe follows the migrating herd of caribou. The halt, the blind, the inept are not left behind, sealed up in a cave or igloo as before; now they're provided rides on a sledge or a travois and are taken along. So, what rules our Western culture is not survival, but rather the second law of human nature. That law is to meet our wants and needs with a minimum expenditure of time, effort, and energy —in other words, to make things as easy as possible for ourselves. An examination of the makeup of our gross national product is most revealing. The bulk of our output is not meeting real needs. Instead it is satisfying demands for effete time- and labor-saving devices, such as electric toothbrushes and instant hot shaving suds.

As a consequence of this second law, we are all inclined to take shortcuts. We can usually get away with this in our private lives. Similarly, if we paint, write, compose, sculpt, or otherwise perform solitary acts to win our bread, we can get by with such a subjective approach to our vocation. Renditions of art are expressions of the artist's subjectivity. But we cannot perform subjectively in business management because of our fiduciary responsibilities. Being in management is to other careers like being in commercial aviation is to private flying. If a private pilot decides to take a joyride in his own plane and chooses not to go down the preflight checklist, it's nobody's neck but his own. But a commercial pilot has a fiduciary responsibility to his airline and to his passengers. Even though he may have climbed into the cockpit of that particular plane several thousand times before, he still has to go down the preflight checklist every time, and cover it from A to Z. If he does not, his career will be short, and he'll take a lot of bodies and expensive property with him. Granted, many things are required of managers that are repetitious and boring. But they represent a penalty that has to be paid by managers in exchange for the perquisites of their positions.

Thoroughness

After clearing our minds of extraneous matter we come to the second component of objectivity — thoroughness. A subjective manager, following the second law of human nature, takes shortcuts. Examining problem situations, he discerns that B has followed A, C has followed B, and D has followed C. Invoking his experience too early, he says to himself, "I've been down this track before." And he comes up with a subjective snap judgment. Contrary to his expectation that all the components of previous situations are going to apply, somewhere around LMNOP, or PQRST, the factors frequently change. And, our shoot-from-the-hip, subjective manager has come up with a decision that will have to be changed. Meanwhile, time, money, image, prestige, and other things may have been lost, perhaps irretrievably. A thorough, objective manager never makes judgments from just part of the facts. He refrains from cooking up answers until everything that belongs in the pot is there, and he sees to it that there are no shortcut exclusions or omissions. He is thorough, recognizing and sublimating the inclination to obey the second law of human nature.

Suppose a subjective manager is feeling poorly and goes to a doctor to find out the reason. The doctor is also subjective and takes shortcuts. He takes a look at the manager's bloodshot eyes, his waxy ears, and his coated tongue and says he has an ulcer. The manager is not likely to accept such a quick diagnosis. He will want a thorough examination — X ray, fluoroscopy, EKG, blood and urine analysis, and so forth. Yet such a subjective manager consistently pardons himself for taking similar shortcuts in diagnosis as he goes about his professional concerns. He habitually takes the easy way out for himself through his obedience to the second law of human nature, and consequently performs badly in carrying out his fiduciary managerial responsibilities.

There is room for expedience in lower or technical management. There are times when it helps to have someone around who can patch up the line with spit, string, and chewing gum and get it moving again to fulfill delivery commitments or meet deadlines. But this capability is usually limiting in nature. To be useful it has to be kept close to the line, so the possessor of this fire-fighting approach is unlikely to be very upwardly mobile.

And managerial people who consistently take the expedient route most often do so not because they have a problem-solving talent, but because they are looking for the easy way out. Being an eager-beaver fire fighter, always the first one up the ladder with the hose, may take a person as far as the chief's car with the bullhorn. But ambitious people who want to make it big back at fire headquarters and become commissioner or deputy commissioner do not do so by fire fighting. Instead, they address themselves to fire prevention, which requires forward planning and anticipation, not expedience.

Anticipation

This brings us to the third component of business objectivity—anticipation. An objective manager looks ahead. He calculates the future impact and import of what he is deciding and doing today. He takes the extra time required to come up with the right and best answer to the problem, one that will stand the test of time. He does not use subjective, shortcut expediencies that get the problems off his back fastest, in observance of the second law of human nature. He sublimates his subjectivity, and instead proceeds objectively to find the best long-range solution to the problem. This approach may take a little longer initially, but in the end it will provide not only the best but also the fastest answer, one that will last and not have to be revised or redone. Thus, more time, effort, and money will not have to be spent in revising the decision or finding a new one. Sometimes, after making a commitment, it is difficult, if not impossible, to manage a change of course. So the objective manager tries to anticipate, and to make the right decision the first time. He operates with an eye to the future, instead of with the here-and-now task orientation of the subjective manager.

The objective, anticipatory manager patrols his area, fire extinguisher at the ready, watching the horizons for wisps of smoke. As he spots them he moves quickly to put the fire out while it is still small — to prevent a brush fire from becoming a forest fire or a broom-closet blaze from reducing an entire building to ashes and rubble. That objective manager would do more than put out the fire; with his anticipation and fire-prevention approach, he would see to it as far as humanly possible that no fire ever occurred there again. The course of a well-run operation is not all ups and downs, peaks and troughs. These waves are minimized and smoothed to mere ripples through objective anticipation and forward planning.

Flexibility

The fourth component of managerial objectivity is flexibility. Most of us spend the first twenty years or so of our lives acquiring a formal education. We then enter business and spend the next twenty years evolving a managerial style. Dozens of books have been written delineating hundreds of such styles. What most of these represent is another shortcutting tactic in response to the second law of human nature. To make it easier on ourselves, we try to come up with a standard unilateral approach to everything. Instead of taking the time and trouble to make an individualized diagnosis and then prescribe and administer the specific therapy needed to correct or cure the problem, we attempt to come up with an all-purpose cure-all—a panacea or placebo.

The older a person becomes and the longer he makes a habit of using a unilateral, stylized approach, the more inflexible he becomes. He may get by with such an ingrained Johnny-one-note style if he continues to practice it in the same work environment in which he evolved it. But, should he ever leave that environment for another, this rigid stance may no longer apply or be all that good a fit for the new circumstances. In many cases of a changed work environment, the inflexible manager begins to perceive that his unilateral approach is not working out well, and he becomes uneasy. But rather than consider alternatives, he comes down harder and stronger with his habitual approach, attempting to bend the circumstances, the problem, and even the company practices and policy to fit his single style.

The reason most men over forty who have lost their jobs and are trying to resituate have difficulty is that it is widely recognized that as a group they have become rigid creatures of habit in their managerial styles. Unless that style happens to fit the work environment they are trying to enter, and the odds are long against such coincidence, they are not going to be of help with the problems. Instead, they are going to be a problem. Men over forty rationalize and make excuses for themselves, blaming their misfortune on the young insurance actuaries who have arbitrarily come up with the number forty for their own calculation purposes. But the forty-and-over predicament is frequently self-induced and usually deserved. Inflexibility of managerial style and the concomitant development of an easy-on-the-user, all-purpose unilateral approach to all problems are the causes. These men look for the easiest, not the best, solutions to problems.

The objective manager, regardless of age, does what is required of him by the circumstances confronting him. He does not require the circumstances to conform to his rigid needs and approaches. He manages by options and alternatives, always having plans B and C at hand and ready to put into the breach if plan A proves ineffective. A subjective manager might be given a mission to gain entry to a building. Over the years he has formed the habit of going to the front door. Sometimes that door is swinging wide open, so entry is easy. Other times the door is ajar, so entry is still easy. And sometimes the door is shut; then the handle merely needs to be turned. When that front door is bolted, locked, chained, and barred, the single-approach subjective manager takes an ax to it and starts to do battle. A flexible, objective manager would back off and case the premises, looking for alternatives. Maybe there is an open back door or side window; maybe he can do some porch climbing or second-story work to get in. He would be thinking objectively about his mission, which is to gain entry into the building, not to defeat the door.

A few more words on flexibility. The sphere is the most prevalent shape in nature. We see it all around us, telescopically, microscopically, and submicroscopically. And we like to think of ourselves and describe ourselves as "nicely rounded spheres." But we must be careful that our spheres are not rigidly round. If we're completely inflexible and brittle we might just shatter somewhere as we encounter an immovable obstacle in our career course. What we need to do is to go back to our high school biology and consider the amoeba. There is much we can learn from that unicellular animal. When it is a perfect round it is static, going nowhere, and accomplishing nothing. When it comes out of its round and sticks out a pseudopod to grab and engulf a piece of food, it is viable and in action. The same pertains when it sticks out another pseudopod to grab a projection of some kind to pull itself in another direction. The amoeba, in other words, only survives and prospers by moving out of its rigid round. Do the same. Be flexible.

To recapitulate: The components of business objectivity are an open-minded, neutral, and thorough diagnostic approach to problems, and the use of anticipation, flexibility, and thoroughness in prescribing optional solutions.

MAKEUP OF BUSINESS PERSONNEL

Three classes of people make up the business population: workers, proprietors, and professional managers. The first two groups are essentially putters-in and takers-out.

Blue-Collar Workers

At the lower end of the scale of the business population are the blue-collar workers, the people on the line. The second law of human nature makes them want to put in a minimum of energy and effort, and to take out a maximum in wages. They collectivize their clout through unions to blackmail greater participation in the company's increased productivity, even when the increase comes from capital expenditure or from technological improvement rather than from greater input on the workers' part. In fact, many unions arbitrarily set unrealistically low standards of production. Regardless of the rhetorical reasons for this practice, it is another instance of a group obeying the second law of human nature.

To the average worker on the line, all the people upstairs in offices are adversaries. The line person usually doesn't want to be concerned about the fiscal and other problems with which the bosses are wrestling. He couldn't care less. In fact, he usually doesn't even want to know or hear about them. All he wants to know about are more paid holidays, longer vacations, earlier full retirement, and more bucks in the pay envelope for less and less performance on his part. Such a line person is frequently a product of a philosophy of child raising that has been widely popular for two generations. In his early life he was not taught discipline, responsibility, or even involvement. All his subjective failings and foibles were forgiven by permissive parents who were afraid of warping his development and personality if they exercised discipline or denial. As a consequence, he was not only indulged, he was spoiled rotten. He became excessively self-centered, subjective, and selfish, with no awareness of the need for objective reality in the work world.

Objective reality requires group teamwork, group cooperation, group involvement, group concern — all antithetical to his loner, selfish attitude. Yet this line person will frequently regard his place of employ as an extension of his home environment, and his boss as a surrogate father. He expects the same permissive forgivings for his failings on the job as he received from his parents, of whom he also took advantage. In other words, he is convinced he has God-given rights to which he is entitled by birth, and he automatically regards his employing company as some sort of extension of the welfare state, whose only reason for being is to take care of him and his needs.

This kind of person expects the railroad to keep running trains regularly and at frequent intervals past his station, even though he rarely rides them, they are empty most of the time, and they lose money every time they leave the yards. Why? Because he may want to ride that train one day when his car breaks down. He regards this kind of insurance as one of his rights, due him regardless of cost to anybody else. He is too self-centered to consider other people.

About fifteen years ago New York City had four newspapers with about five years of back-to-back increasing losses. Their three-year contracts were up for renewal, and the papers pleaded for mercy. In response, they were clobbered by the biggest package of union demands ever. The newspapers were forced to shut down. The consternation was unbelievable. Wires, letters, and phone calls to the president, the New York State governor, and the mayor had one message — "You can't do this to us. How are we going to survive without following the daily doings of Orphan Annie? We've got rights. Those papers can't shut down. It mustn't be allowed." How out of touch with reality! Yet, downwardly to this unbelievable group is the direction in which most subjective managers relate. They want to be good bosses, to win popularity contests, to be good shepherds to their flocks, to relate nostalgically to their origins.

Proprietors

At the upper end of the business totem pole is the other group of putters-in and takers-out. These are the owners, who are putting in their money and want to take out a profit. They are not interested in winning awards for the best-designed widget if it doesn't sell profitably. They are not interested in being noted for having the most sunlit and sanitary premises in the industry, air-conditioning, and Muzak around the clock. If these superlative work conditions are going to increase productivity sufficiently to warrant the capital expenditure, fine. That's a good business investment. But for creature comfort alone, no way.

The put-in and take-out owners don't understand the put-in and take-out workers. Understandably, they reason as follows: "Can't those people downstairs realize that if we give them everything they want we'll go broke? How long can we keep going down this one-way street, without getting anything in return, before we lose our competitive position in the marketplace and have to shut down the operation? Don't they understand that what keeps those wheels on the line turning is profitability, which these line guys are doing their best to wipe out? Without profit, how can we invest in better marketing, improved production technology, even just replacement equipment? They're killing the goose that lays the golden eggs."

Professional Managers

Interposed between the diametrically opposed viewpoints of the two put-in and take-out groups is the third class of person to be found in business — the professional manager. Managers must act as referees, buffers, insulators, and coordinators. They must do everything they can to reconcile these different approaches so that the operation will make a profit in spite of everything and everybody. And the more profit, the better. If they don't make a profit, or enough profit, these professional managers will be replaced, individually or as a team, by the owners. The owners will continue the process until someone does make a satisfactory profit or they become convinced that nobody can. In the latter case they will then take their money out and put it elsewhere, in order to take a reasonable profit.

The point of all this is to set the record straight. The subjective manager, from his task orientation, his downward relating to his level of entry, his workingman's philosophy, is directing his attention incorrectly. From below he will get nothing but grief. The blessings — the raises, rewards, and recognitions — flow from above. So it behooves the professional manager to relate and accommodate upwardly in order to maximize his career, recognizing that the superior is not there to take care of his subordinates; the subordinates are there to take care of their superiors. And he realizes his company is not an extension of the welfare state. If it is to stay in business, it must make a profit judged adequate by the owners, regardless of any other consideration, such as people in the company's employ.

Because of the problems they cause, workers are understandably held in low regard by many owners, and are often deservedly viewed as just so much necessary production equipment, nuisances to be phased out and replaced when obsolescence sets in. Meanwhile, many owners, if only as retaliation against the problems they cause, frequently give workers preventive maintenance and no more. They're kept clean, oiled, and in good working order only. Anything beyond that is resented and begrudged as undeserved because of minimal performance, negative or obstructive attitude, and complete lack of understanding of business reality and the problems of management.

Deciding Where
You Should Work

If you have ever been in the military, you may have noticed how much it resembles business and vice versa. This is not mere coincidence; business deliberately began copying the military many centuries ago.

Armies and navies began essentially as the playthings of royalty, used as human chessmen by kings, dukes, princes, and lords in their war games. Members of the military willingly accepted the risks involved because if they became proficient at their martial profession there was no faster way to honor, acclaim, prestige, and money, despite the handicap of low birth. In fact, in those early days the only way for ambitious, courageous men to escape the almost insurmountable limitations of humble origin was to seek a career in the military, with prowess at arms the vehicle to position.

The same motivation prompts today's underprivileged but ambitious kids to escape from ghettos by so excelling at a particular sport that they get athletic scholarships through high school and college and perhaps lucrative offers from the pros upon graduation. After their playing days are over, they are still relatively young and they can usually enter some business at a fairly high level because their names and fame can be useful far beyond the discipline they graduated in. They very frequently become front men, serving in a public relations or customer relations capacity while living very well at company expense.

When man was no longer a nomad hunter, settling instead in one spot and learning to till and live off the land, he had the time and stability to develop other skills and crafts. Some became potters, others weavers, others carvers, smiths, weapons-makers, and so forth. Such people bartered their produce for wheat, meat, wine, wool, and other necessities. But they soon saturated their local village market, and had to expand the radius of their marketplace to include neighboring villages.

The arrangement was not entirely satisfactory to most artisans of the time. It meant they had to leave their beloved potters' wheels, or looms, or forges, and go on the road. And going on the road in those days was quite dangerous, not an undertaking for those who were faint of heart or unskilled in the use of arms, as the countryside was infested with robbers, brigands, highwaymen, and assorted other opportunists who preyed on the wayfarer.

Many of the predators were military men between engagements, or ex-military men who knew only one trade well — the martial. They were risk takers, which the craftsmen were not. They were conditioned to the rigors of travel; they understood and knew from experience how to cope with the perils of attempted passage through a strange countryside, all things largely unknown to the stay-at-home artisans.

After centuries of raidings and robbings the inevitable happened. The military-entrepreneurial predators gradually went legitimate. They joined forces with the craftsmen. The militarists-turned-entrepreneur bought the produce of groups of artisans, who could now stay happily and safely at home, plying their craft. Sometimes the entrepreneurs acted as the agents or means of delivery for a share of the proceeds. Either way, the militaristic risk takers became line people and got the greater rewards. The behind-the-scenes stay-at-home artisans became staff and got lesser rewards—a satisfactory and equitable arrangement for them, as they were taking no personal risks.

The line people organized their convoying along familiar military lines. They knew they would frequently have to fight to keep their cargoes, whether outbound or inbound. They borrowed the military gradations of rank, military chain of command, military training and procedural manuals for the field escort forces, and military tactics and strategy for the protection and safe delivery of their goods to the known markets and back.

As time went on and production increased, the line entrepreneurs began to expand their radius of operation by attacking less well-known, or even strange, markets. This penetrating effort required further strategy, campaign effort, and organization, again all predicated on military rules and experience. And from a single pack train, caravan, wagon train, or shipload, deliveries grew to become fleet and multiple operations; one group of line entrepreneurs might have dozens of expeditions under way simultaneously to many widely separated markets.

In the beginning, trade was irregular, often a one-shot deal. This take-it-while-it-is-available approach worked satisfactorily in the relatively nearby markets, where people understood the product and its use. But to develop a distant market by creating a demand for a new product took some convincing, some salesmanship. People were not about to change their life-styles, abandoning the use of a long-familiar item for something different even if it was better unless they could be certain of being able to obtain more of the product. This form of resistance could only be overcome by an assured regular supply.

The line entrepreneur had to think beyond being merely a conveyor or convoyer of what was available on a random basis. He came back from his trips and began to pay some attention to production, organizing it so as to be certain of the constant volume he needed. In turn he became involved in procurement and personnel in order to come by needed raw material and people trained to process it. Next came the problem of satisfying a greater demand volume than could be produced manually. So the entrepreneur got into simple mechanization, and ultimately into our current sophisticated technology and administrative methodology.

Today line and staff roles in large businesses are becoming more equal in importance; in fact, the importance is sometimes even reversed. Successful field commanders always enjoyed greater rewards than did officers in the quartermaster corps, concerned with materiel and logistics. Large corporations by their size and weight require a huge support structure, with compartmentation and delegation, all achieved by staff people. The man at the top is a long way from the firing line. The line people out in the field report back to and through the staff people who populate corporate headquarters and are constantly present. The staff people have easier access to the ears of top command, and the word that reaches those ears has been buffered, filtered, and even altered outright. Negatives are frequently watered down or even omitted completely, while positives are embellished and polished before presentation upward.

Many times the top man never gets an accurate picture. He hears what the staff chooses to report to him. Quite naturally the slanting of and tampering with facts will be done to make the staff look good and more important. The staff will deliberately minimize contributions made by line people from a feeling of competition and from efforts to catch up with line, which historically has been on top in both the military and business hierarchies.

Thus, there is less room and need today for line people in large corporations. The heyday of the hotshot, personality guy, pro salesman, and sales manager types is over. Marketing is no longer idiosyncratic and individualized, but is rather a group corporate function. It is handled mostly by staff people from the purveying company dealing with their staff equivalents at the purchasing companies, with field men performing mere service and trouble-shooting functions. Missionary and educational work is done through national advertising put together by corporate staffs. Market research and new product development are handled back at headquarters by means of mathematical models and simulations run, through the computer by staffers before any field testing takes place.

So, the staff function is now assuming greater importance in large corporations than is that of the line, and entrepreneurial line people are not that compatible to such an operation, nor is the operation that compatible to them. Because of size, weight, and structure the large corporation moves too slowly for action-oriented line people. Staffers are usually empire preservers, rather than empire builders, with strong security needs having priority over taking risks. Heavy capital investment in existing plants and equipment also slows down changes. Staff caution, inertia, and reluctance to make waves and rock the boat also get in the way of activist, chance-taking line people.

Entrepreneurially oriented persons should avoid trying to find careers in very large corporations. Organization needs as viewed and interpreted by the large numbers of staff people aboard transcend all other needs, especially those of the entrepreneur. And it doesn't matter how well a person can do a job, or how well he or she is paid. If a person is not happy in his particular work environment he or she does not have a career, or even a job, but a jail sentence. For the same reason that happiness is what makes for a career, compatibility, rather than competence or compensation, is the keynote. Security-minded, structured staff types who don't like to take chances should seek employment with very large corporations and avoid smaller, swinging, unstructured, volatile work environments that would provide the kind of climate in which entrepreneurs thrive.

In the work environment of a smaller company a planning meeting is held sometime before the close of the fiscal year. At this meeting, after the review of the past year has been made, the executive officer chairing the meeting will ask the vice president of sales, "How many of our widgets do you think we can sell next year?" The vice president of sales will reply, "My gut reaction is to project sales of a half-million."

The executive officer then approaches the vice president of production: "What are we going to need in the way of additional production facilities to turn out a half-million widgets next year?" The reply comes back: "We'll need another dozen framisses and a half-dozen razzmatazzes, but we haven't got room for them in our present plant. We'll have to house them elsewhere." The chairman says to the vice president of personnel, "What about framis and razzmatazz operators? Will we have problems finding fifty or sixty more?" The reply is, "We've pretty much drained off the local market but there are plenty around the Southeast and Midwest we can bring in."

After these conversations the executive officer says, "Since we are penetrating the Midwest market pretty heavily and it still represents our greatest near-term potential for further growth, maybe we should think about opening a branch plant in or closer to that market. Lower freight from a shorter distance will make us more competitive. And we can find needed plant people locally rather than having to pay a lot of relocation expenses." The executive officer–chairman turns to the vice president of procurement: "Can our present sources of supply provide the additional volume of raw materials we'll need to turn out a half-million widgets?" The reply is, "No, we'll have to find some new sources. There are several in the Midwest we should be able to tap."

And so it goes. Everything hinges on the educated guesstimate of the vice president of sales. If he has overestimated, the company's in bad trouble, stuck with a loss and unneeded people, plant, production, raw material, sources, and so forth. If he has underestimated, there is still trouble, although it is not as serious. To meet sales volume beyond the half-million widgets it is geared to produce may require heavy production overtime, premium prices for the additional raw materials needed, and so forth. The whole costing system would be disrupted, and overall profit diminished.

The entire atmosphere is quite different from that found in king-size companies. All the people in this smaller environment are entrepreneurial, or should be to be comfortable, effective, and happy. The biggest risk taker of them all is the old-fashioned, fly-by-the-seat-of-his-pants vice president of sales. His prognostication of half a million widgets had better be right, and right on target.

Otherwise, everybody else's planning and implementation are based on an incorrect premise, and the whole operation has a plethora of interlocking problems that will be difficult to resolve because of their inseparability. Staff people are quite unhappy in such a precarious, fast-and-loose environment. Line people love it.

Decide which type you are and pick your setting accordingly so that you can have a meaningful and happy career. If you're in the wrong environment for your makeup and psychology, your uncertainty, discomfort, and unhappiness will not only impair your work effectiveness, they will cause physical reactions. Your frustrations and inner turmoil could easily result in alcoholism, ulcers, circulatory disorders, or a cardiac condition. And you might come home nights to find yourself venting your anger and frustration by kicking the dog, yelling at the kids, and fighting with your spouse. There are no vacuums in nature and matters must eventually balance out. If there is a cause there will be an effect, and an action will be followed by a reaction. So aside from learning how to do your thing, give a lot of thought and attention to where you will do it.

Interpersonal Skills

The bulk of our communication, especially at work, is of necessity verbal. Most of us use tact and diplomacy and try to be nice guys, but the second law of human nature also makes its presence felt. We are inclined to take shortcuts and to use handy, convenient words for ease of transmission. The language is replete with expressions that rationalize this subjective approach. "I tell it like it is," "I don't mince words," "I call a spade a spade," and "I lay it on the line."

Unfortunately, this shortcut approach to communications problems has unhappy results. Listeners may not perceive our good intentions and may interpret our words quite differently from what we had in mind. They may react defensively to what we said with that shortcut directness. And when people become defensive, a psychological syndrome sets in.

An early manifestation of this syndrome is that communications stop. The listener's hearing aid gets turned off. Any later softening of the impact or logical explanation is not heard, and is therefore lost. The final manifestation of this syndrome is the need to retaliate, and this need is ineradicable. Retaliate the listener will, no matter how long it takes him. Retaliation is not necessarily overt. The listener will not catch the offender in a dark alley some moonless night and punch his nose. Any business environment provides dozens of covert opportunities daily for a defensive person to even the score, to retaliate indirectly but effectively.

No manager can afford this kind of retaliation. It can greatly affect his career. The fact that he has reached his exalted position does not mean that somewhere en route he has picked up additional sensory equipment to help him. He still has only two eyes with their limited peripheral vision, not radar or other electronic scanning devices. He still has only two ears, not a rotating disk antenna for auditory apparatus. To discharge his managerial duties he needs help and advance intelligence from willing volunteers manning his watchtowers and listening posts.

The manager mentioned earlier, who anticipates trouble, who patrols the grounds, fire extinguisher in hand, might start moving toward a wisp of smoke he discerns on the horizon, intent on getting that fire out before it really starts to blaze. But unknown to him, something dire may be overtaking him from the rear. He may be about to get clobbered. At this point he needs somebody around him to yell, "Look out behind you!" and perhaps to throw his body in the way, to intercept, to slow down the impending disaster long enough to give him a chance to turn around and cope. If he is surrounded by people whom he has made defensive and retaliatory by direct communication, nobody is going to warn or intercept. Instead, everyone is going to sit still, look on silently, and savor watching him get clobbered. This is a passive form of retaliation, something no manager can afford if he hopes to have a career.

How can we avoid this situation? By rephrasing our messages in such a way that they will be received and perceived without the recipient(s) becoming defensive and retaliatory. This does not mean we cop out, telling people only what they want to hear, rather than what they need to hear. It is our method of communicating that is important. We cannot use the words that are most convenient and easiest for us. Instead of proceeding so subjectively we have to think of what we are trying to convey from the standpoint of the listener and make the necessary adjustments.

A direct communicator might say to an associate, "Joe, you're a damned liar." Off Joe will go on the defensive retaliatory syndrome. Had the direct communicator rethought the matter and the message he might have said instead, "Joe, I envy you. You have a marvelously vivid imagination that comes on in living color, whereas mine is just plain old black and white. And you have another quality I wish I had more of, and that's your enthusiasm. But there are times, Joe, when your imagination and enthusiasm incline you to overstate."

The same message has been conveyed, but in words that are acceptable to the listener. The communicator has placed the listener in a superior position by envying his greater imagination and enthusiasm. The listener's reaction in all likelihood will be, "He's right. I do get overly worked up a lot of times and run off at the mouth. I'm going to have to watch that. He's a good guy for drawing it to my attention, and I owe him a favor in return." Instead of a defensive and retaliatory person on his hands, the communicator now has someone in his debt, and an IOU he can cash in later.

Here is another example. A man is managing an area of an operation. He has a peer neighbor managing an adjacent area of the operation that the first man knows a good deal about. That peer neighbor is doing a very poor job. But our first man is a nice guy, so he bides his time, bites his tongue, and says nothing for a long time. However, one day he has had a bellyful, so he bounces over to his neighbor and says, "Joe, when in the hell are you going to stop this idiocy and start running your operation like this—*da de da de da de da?*" Joe doesn't hear the *da de da*'s. His hearing aid was turned off fast as he reacted defensively. He perceives the first man as highly critical, a superior wise guy, singling him out, putting him out on a limb, and taking pot shots at him. He may require three or four comebacks before he feels the score has been evened. His retaliation was earned by the shortcut direct communication, even though the criticism was long overdue, delayed, and deserved.

Had the first manager been objective, he might have said instead, "Joe, I've been wondering about something. Some years back when I was with the ABC Company we had the same kind of problem we are having here in your end of our operation. They found that by *da de da de da de da* they got the same happy result we're looking for. No way am I trying to tell you what to do, Joe. I just thought I'd mention what ABC did, so that you could give it some thought and maybe even a try."

Obviously, Joe's reaction is not going to be defensive and retaliatory. The second manager did not criticize Joe. He identified by using all the editorial plurals, rather than by singling Joe out. He did not claim or infer that the *da de da* solution was his idea, even though it may have been. In no way can Joe believe that the ABC Company never had such a problem or that it never could have solved it by going the *da de da* route. He cannot claim that his brain is superior to the collective brains of the ABC Company. His only reaction can be to think that the first manager was observant while he was with the ABC Company, that he has a good memory, and that he is trying to help by relating the ABC experience. Joe has no choice but to try the ABC way. He's been painted into a corner. He's been manipulated by the first manager, and he doesn't mind at all. In fact, he likes it and is grateful.

Avoiding direct communication in a subjective manner and thereby avoiding making people defensive and retaliatory separates the users from the used. This interpersonal skill creates manipulators. Some of the worst bastards encountered in business understand the need not to make people around them defensive, and so

32

rephrase their messages. As a consequence, and as a fringe benefit, while they proceed ruthlessly toward their own career-betterment ends, they are perceived by their associates as being very nice guys. They haven't made anyone defensive and retaliatory.

Perhaps this rephrasing effort appears to be too time consuming, like going around Robin Hood's barn, but it is worth the trouble. Tact and diplomacy are practiced ostensibly for the sake of the other guy, but under the test of stress and pressure, nice guys blow their cool like everyone else who is operating in a subjective manner. Rephrasing avoids much crisis and confrontation, and enables the person practicing it to retain his or her composure in emergencies, and to look good by comparison. The effort is worthwhile. It is not being made for the sake of someone else or for the sake of being perceived as a nice guy — it is being done coldly and objectively to advance one's own career.

I am sure every reader has a large enough vocabulary to rephrase if he or she is willing to try. In the beginning, habitual direct communicators may find this awkward. But this is temporary, akin to learning a new language. In the beginning they'd have to think in English, and then translate into French, German, or Italian. With time and practice, they'd be able to think originally in that other language, and time to translate would be obviated.

It is somewhat like learning to play golf. Everything is disjointed and done by the numbers at first, with a lot of horrible hacking ensuing. How do I take my grip and stance? How much do I flex my knees? How much do I bend over? How do I start the club back, and where do I stop? How do I start down and finish? With time and practice the swing becomes grooved. Instinct and habit take over; forethought is no longer required.

I can now concentrate on shotmaking. How do I finesse my way around this layout? How do I avoid the hazards and trouble? Here I am with a tree in the way of my next shot. Do I open up a nine iron or wedge and loft the ball over? Do I close the face of a two or three iron and knock the ball under the tree onto the green? Once I've made up my mind about the shot to make I needn't worry about its execution—I just hit the ball.

Rephrasing poses similar problems, except that you don't have to go out to the golf course or driving range to groove your swing. You can practice anytime anywhere so long as there are other human beings in your presence. It doesn't matter who or what they are. They can be barbers, bartenders, waiters, waitresses, cab drivers, bus drivers, or elevator or newsstand operators. Practice rephrasing your communications so that nobody becomes defensive and retaliatory.

Other aspects of objectivity are to be used exclusively on the job, like a hard hat, hard-toed shoes, a flak suit, or other protective gear. When you come off the job, take these off and leave them in your locker. Go home your own sweet subjective self. Nobody wants to be married to, or socialize with, a humanoid computer. But the interpersonal skill of never making people defensive is something you should use everywhere, 24 hours a day, 365 days a year. Using this skill will enrich a lot of other lives besides your own. You are now privy to a priceless secret — one that will enable you to become a manipulator instead of one of the manipulated.

Communications

HOW TO COMMUNICATE WITH
AND RELATE TO THE BOSS

An ambitious and objective professional manager has to show whose side he is on, and that side is not below him, but above. He must relate upwardly, he must think of the owners, and think like the owners, to be successful in his upward mobility aspirations. Ordinarily he will not have direct access to the owners or even to top management. The military-like chain of command is there for his use, however. His pipeline into the system, his upward line of communication, is through his boss. An objective manager has to demonstrate that he knows not only the name, but also the rules, of the game he is playing if he hopes to come up a winner. Just as if he were in the military, he accommodates to his superior, and does everything in his power to assist the man above. He recognizes that his mission is to make his boss's job as easy as possible.

How does he accomplish his mission? First of all, he lets his boss know what he is doing at all times, not just verbally, but in periodic written reports. There may be an organizational reporting methodology. Such reports are frequently directed elsewhere, or become too fragmented. The boss does not get the full story, or he gets it too late.

Suppose the boss's boss comes to him and asks what one of his subordinates is doing. The boss has to confess, "I don't really know. He's off in his corner doing something in his area. I've been traveling and have been busy with other matters, so I haven't had a chance to talk to him for several weeks." Both boss and subordinate become suspect because they have been guilty of poor communications.

Worse yet, the boss's boss charges up with fire in his eyes and says, "What's this I hear about So-and-So (one of the boss's subordinates) dicing kumquats? Whoever told him to do that ought to be fired." Maybe the boss didn't know So-and-So was dicing kumquats. Then again, maybe he did. But the boss may be fiscally or psychologically unwilling to take a stance, to defend that subordinate by admitting he knew he was dicing kumquats. Besides, he may not be that impressed by the subordinate's performance because the subordinate does not relate upwardly so he really doesn't care if So-and-So stays or goes. He might very well say, "I didn't know he was dicing kumquats. It must be his own idea." So-and-So is left holding the bag. If he tries arguing the point by saying the boss knew, he's not going to win. It is his word against the boss's, and the boss has the greater clout and credibility.

So wherever you are, start communicating with your boss in written form. You will protect yourself and him from above, and yourself from him. How often to submit these reports depends on the work situation. If the climate is placid and slow moving, once a month may be enough. If the environment changes quickly, twice a month might be necessary. If the climate is really dynamic, a job-shop kind of operation, once a week reporting may be required.

Do not write at length, as you would back in high school trying to pass English Composition II. Strip out all the adverbs and adjectives, using only nouns and verbs. Do not describe ongoing, housekeeping matters. Confine yourself to changes — changes in policy, procedure, personnel, and projects. Report such changes and projects completed and begun in cable-ese, as if you were writing a telegram or night letter.

Send additional copies for your boss's routing convenience. Do not presume to mark these for routing for him or around him. Leave them blank for him to mark and route as he sees fit. Simply provide the additional copies he may want, as your assuming the routing prerogatives would be in contravention of the chain of command. To protect yourself, you do have the right to route copies to several of your peers and key subordinates.

Your boss can no longer claim that he didn't know you were dicing kumquats. You didn't get a fast cease-and-desist from him, which means you had tacit approval to go ahead. He is now involved and can't cop out when somebody higher than him asks, "How come he's dicing kumquats?" He's got to protect you, and the heat is off. You're surviving. If you can just do that, you are bound to prosper to some extent, if only through attrition. It would be unrealistic for the boss to claim he didn't get your memo when everybody else did. The mere fact that you routed copies to your peers and subordinates is going to discourage his going the disclaimer route.

Americans, unlike businessmen elsewhere in our Western technological society, generally rely entirely too much on the verbal for their internal business communications. And the phone is entirely too handy, with Ma Bell certainly encouraging its use. Despite this, we're still suffering from a paper blizzard, although most of it is caused by government-required reporting of one kind or another. As a possible overreaction to this excessive paperwork, we seem to avoid internal written communications. This lack of documentation has all kinds of unfavorable results. We invariably confirm in writing any external verbal communications. We don't accept or give orders in person or over the phone without written confirmation. That would be highly unbusinesslike. In turn, we expect written acknowledgment of receipt of our orders, stating terms, prices, shipping dates, and so forth. And we write letters confirming our phone conversations. We need that protection, that insurance, both for the sake of our company and for the sake of the company with whom we are doing business. There seems to be no quarrel with this practice. It is a nationally accepted method of conduct, an understood way of relating with other companies.

Peculiarly, the same manager who carefully protects himself and his company in his outside dealings by written communication or confirmation, will leave himself wide open and vulnerable in his internal dealings by a too heavy reliance on the verbal. There may be many reasons for this neglect of the written form. He may feel safe and secure. He may not choose to make the effort because of his observance of the second law of human nature. He may feel he's too busy to bother. He may not want to seem all that different when nobody else bothers to write. He may trust his associates too much and feel that he doesn't need protection. At any rate he does not put enough into writing in-house.

This neglect can be highly dangerous. As we've said before, you've got to survive in management before you can prosper. You can't leave yourself wide open as fall guy for your associates. In fact, you've got to protect yourself more within the organization than externally in your business dealings if you want to stay aboard, survive, and eventually prosper. Better to err on the too much side than on the too little. Do not try to slide by on the spoken word alone. Get it on paper.

The language is replete with expressions derogating the auditory — "In one ear and out the other," "It's only hearsay," "You can't believe everything you hear," and so forth. Conversely, everything that appears in print is popularly thought to have had divine editing — "Seeing is believing," "There it was in black and white," and the like. The highest avowal of truth that can be made is, "I saw it with my own eyes." Keep in mind the relative attitudes toward, and the credibilities of, the auditory versus the visual. Talk less and write more. If talk has to precede the written word, be sure to confirm. Practice some of the components of objectivity; be thorough and anticipatory in the all-important area of communications. You'll not only appear professional, you'll be safe.

Next run a profile on your boss. Find out what he is all about and how he got to be that way. He is never going to be 100 percent objective, no more than you or anybody else. Being 100 percent objective is a physical impossibility. Our own neurology and physiology prevent it. But if you can find out where his on and off buttons are, what makes him tick, what makes him growl, what makes him purr, you can accommodate yourself to him better. You might learn that he needs four cups of coffee and doesn't begin to cerebrate until 10 o'clock. You'll know enough not to buttonhole him at two minutes after 9 o'clock some morning before he's even gotten his hat and coat off. You'll wait to tell him about the great idea you've lain awake all night dreaming up. You'll realize you're apt to get a cool, noncomprehending reception or maybe even a rebuff or rejection. You will have learned to sublimate your subjective need to communicate at the earliest possible moment. You'll wait until after 10 o'clock.

In fact, you may have learned that the boss is at his ebullient, receptive best at about 1:30 in the afternoon, after he's come back from a lunch preceded by two martinis. If so, that's when you introduce your brainchild to him. By the same token, you may have learned that he runs out of gas in the late afternoon, so you never bring up anything important after 4 o'clock. Instead, you wait until the next day after 10 o'clock. There is much you can add to this profile through observation. To get started, take a look at *Who's Who* or your company's annual report.

One ideal method is to go to the person in charge of personnel. Explain that your mission is to relate to and accommodate your boss. To perform your mission better and faster, you'd like to know where he came from, what his early life was like, where he went to school, what his family is like, where he worked before, and so forth. The personnel chief will be happy to oblige. He'll be flattered by your approach and understanding. Personnel people are frequently held in low regard by their work associates, whether line or staff. He'll appreciate your upgrading of his importance and function. You will not only get the information you are looking for, you will have made a friend and ally.

From the preceding chapter on Interpersonal Skills it should be apparent that running a profile on your boss has one last but most important purpose. Your mission is to accommodate upwardly to your boss. This can hardly be done if you are defensive and retaliatory toward him. Compiling the profile will largely eliminate these feelings. You'll make allowances, take things from whence they come, and recognize the reasons for any subjective behavior the boss manifests. We cannot hope to change him, or anybody else. All we can realistically hope for is to change and control ourselves. Rank has its privileges and we must accord them, even if it means modification on our part. The profile on the boss will make it easier for us to do so. And it will considerably reduce the likelihood of our becoming defensive and retaliatory toward him.

Your functions as a manager, regardless of what you're managing, are to make money and to save money, by solving the problems standing in the way of greater profitability. You do these things with and through your boss, not for or instead of him. The manager who goes to his boss and says "We've got this problem. What do you want to do about it?" is going to have a short career; he is no help. He is apt to be identified as a harbinger of bad news, and bring forth a negative association in his boss's mind. Playing it safe by doing nothing does not help the boss.

Helping the boss can also be overdone. The manager who goes to his boss and says, "Did we ever get clobbered by a problem. But I fixed it. Here's what I did," is going to have an even shorter career than the do-nothing manager. He has rendered his boss unnecessary. He has usurped his boss's prerogatives. He has become a threat to the boss, not a help. The boss will get rid of him quickly.

The knowing objective manager avoids the two extremes. He stays away from the far-out black or white areas of subjectivity and operates in the gray, middle area of objectivity. He goes to his boss and says "We've got this problem. We can go Road A, Route B, or Avenue C. I think we ought to go Road A, but what do you think?" If the boss has learned to trust this manager's judgment, more often than not he'll give the subordinate's recommendation the go-ahead.

The subordinate confirms in writing that as of such and such a date, after alternatives A, B, and C were looked over, Road A was chosen as the best solution to the problem. Getting this confirmation into the written record serves as protection. It gives the boss a chance to monitor against possible misunderstanding or garbling of transmission. And it could protect you in the future, when somebody in higher authority asks the two of you, "What are you guys doing on Road A? Why aren't you on Avenue C or even Turnpike G?" You can now show that you looked at these options and judged Road A to be the best solution. Managers are forgiven an occasional judgmental error, as nobody ever bats 1.000. Managers are not forgiven for being unthorough, for not exploring all alternative solutions to problems.

You and your subordinates may have researched a half-dozen or more options, including Turnpike G. You needn't present all these alternatives to the boss. If you do so, you have rendered yourself unnecessary, as the boss could have gone directly to your subordinates. You should be able to narrow the options down to the best three or four, however many are about equally viable. The possibilities you have culled as being less desirable, including Turnpike G, you keep in your files. You do not present all possible alternatives, only those you judge best.

Nor should you present only one option. That would demonstrate subjective inflexibility, a unilateral stylized approach. Any problem in business or life has more than one solution. Life itself has at least two options — to live or to die. So if you find yourself frequently coming up with only one possible solution to present to the boss, examine your objectivity. You have probably reverted to subjective rigidity in your problem-solving approach.

Every now and then, depending on the boss's psychology and how often he needs to show he is still the boss, he may reject your recommended course from among the several options you have submitted. He might say that he just has a hunch or a gut feeling that Route B is the way to go. Thereupon you say, "Okay, Route B it is." And off you go. But before you implement the solution, write a confirmation so that he has a chance to monitor your understanding or to have second thoughts.

Occasionally you will receive second-hand instructions from a peer who also reports to your boss, and who manages a section of the operation adjacent to yours. He might say that your mutual superior has instructed him to make a change that will require an accommodating alteration at your end, since you are fore or aft of him. You do not run to the boss and question what you've been told. Instead, you confirm these instructions back to the boss in writing. "On such and such a date, as per your instructions relayed to me by So-and-So, we are changing from X to Y."

The boss has a chance to monitor against possible misunderstandings and garbling in transmission. He is also guarded against the possibility that your peer is a grabby guy who is exceeding his authority and usurping the prerogatives of the boss. Better to give the boss the opportunity to nip this in the bud than to have him reproach you later, saying, "Didn't you know better than to make this change without checking with me first?" If you don't, it might be weeks or months before he realizes what has happened. And by then it may be difficult or even impossible to change back. Commitments may have been made to the point of irretrievability, getting everybody into trouble, especially you.

Years ago there was a popular parlor game played by young people. They would sit in a circle. One of them would write a sentence on a pad, and then whisper it in the ear of his or her neighbor. That person would whisper his or her version of what had been heard into the ear of the next person. So it would go, around the circle, until the last hearer, next to the person who had written and started the one-liner, stated aloud his or her final understanding of the message. Naturally, there was little resemblance to the original, and the differences were often ludicrous. Unfortunately, this verbal replay game is heavily played in business, with the same result. In business, however, it is not funny; it is tragic. So write and confirm. Protect everybody — most of all, yourself.

Be of further help to your boss and yourself by committing your ideas for improvement to paper. If you merely tell them to your boss, he restates them to his boss, and that person relays them to someone else, there are too many opportunities for garblings in transmission. Your ideas may have to go up four or five ranks, from a division to a corporate level, before the decision-making point is reached. By the time it gets there, decisions are likely to be made on completely different assumptions and understandings from those you initially postulated.

When you come up with ideas, be objectively thorough in your homework. Don't just come up with the positives—a blue-sky sales pitch. Include the negatives, and show how these can be overcome, if possible. If they can't, don't exclude them; such omissions would make you appear unthorough and unobjective. As long as the positives outweigh the negatives and the net result would be a good deal, write it up and send it to your boss, with extra unmarked copies for his discretionary routing. Your idea will then reach the decision-making level intact and will be judged on merit, not misunderstanding.

This way of going will also protect you against plagiarism. If you just verbalize an idea to your boss he may pooh-pooh it, and you subside. To your discomfiture and dismay, your idea may resurface a year later, only now it comes from your boss and he takes the credit and the glory. If you write up your ideas, with copies to your key peers and subordinates, this can't happen and won't even be attempted.

Another way you can help your boss (and yourself) is by displaying a positive attitude as you proceed with your concerns. Nobody wants pessimistic, negative, hand-wringing apostles of doom and gloom around. The effect is too depressing and too likely to communicate itself to others. Neither can you be an unrealistic, starry-eyed, hope-springs-eternal optimist. A manager's mission is to convert negatives to positives, which is another way of saying that he has to be a problem solver, not a problem creator.

Before he can solve problems, the manager has to recognize them. To do this he has to proceed from a realistic, objective stance, not from one of deliberate oversight, omission, or pretense that there is no problem. He must recognize and tackle his problems in an upbeat fashion, in a positive way, in full and cheerful expectation that he can overcome these challenges, not be beaten by them.

Any business path down which a manager is looking is sure to be strewn with boulders. How he views these is highly important to people in his work environment. Does he regard these boulders as roadblocks or as stepping-stones? Does he proceed negatively or positively? His attitude and the way in which he goes about his concerns are important, as they will rub off on the people around him and influence their performance. Even if he is unsure or insecure, for the morale of his associates and subordinates a manager cannot conduct his affairs as if he were at a wake. He has to play his role, act his part as called for by the script. He must project a positive, confident attitude at all times, rather than display any uncertainty or despondency.

Proceeding about his concerns with a deadpan poker face is not enough, either. The manager must seem cheerful and flex his smile muscles frequently. He is responsible for establishing the climate in his portion of the operation, so he can't come on stormy, cloudy, or even overcast. He has to create a fair, clear, and sunny atmosphere whether he feels that way or not. He has to sublimate his subjective feelings and do what is required of him, which is to provide a favorable working climate for his portion of the operation. Any manager who can do this will be gratefully appreciated by his subordinates, but most especially by his superiors.

Relate to and assist your boss by touting and shilling for him. Any manager needs to make noise, to acquire visibility, to make his presence felt. Tooting his own horn is bad form and unacceptable. People very quickly tire of listening to "I, I, I, how great I am." That first person pronoun "I" is the most reprehensible word in the language, and its use should be limited as much as possible. Talk instead in editorial plurals such as "we," "us," "our." You've never really been that alone, anyway. You'll then be perceived as a team guy rather than as a loner.

Use possessive pronouns like "my" or "mine" in lieu of "I" where you can't invoke editorial plurals. Expressions like "my mission" or "my responsibility" do not grate on the listener's ear and are far better received than "I, I, I." At any rate you can make a lot of noise and get away with it if you are touting your boss rather than yourself. "How great my boss is" is far more acceptable than "How great am I."

As you make a great deal of noise on his behalf, some good will rub off on you. Not only will everyone know you're there, your boss will be very grateful for your help and will want to keep you close by to do more of the same for him. As he gets promoted he'll take you along, usually by tapping you to succeed him as he moves up. With your shoulder under his butt helpfully pushing, plus his own momentum, he might just take off like a big bird. You're promoting him out of your way, you're hitching your wagon to his star, you're riding on his coattails, instead of clawing him off the ladder rung above you.

There is no better way to accelerate your upward mobility, and this route could take you a lot farther than you'd get by your own efforts alone. This kind of behavior will also be noticed by others besides your boss. One of his superiors may decide he'd like to have you shill for him, so he takes advantage of his greater clout and pirates you away. Now you are a peer of your former boss and slated to pass him because you've latched on to a bigger and faster-moving star, or caused that star to latch onto you. There's no way your former boss can impede your progress. Because your new boss is his superior, it would not be politic or circumspect for him even to try.

Your former boss will still be grateful for your help while you were with him. And if you're a comer marked for greater things, he isn't going to spoil your relationship. He may want to come to you later for favors. Meanwhile, he's getting credit for having brought you aboard, for training you, for bringing you along. Surrendering you isn't going to be a total loss to him. He will receive immediate as well as future benefits on the basis of your past relationship. At the same time, you're enjoying your promotion, greater perquisites, and a faster track, all by being politic.

One of the less obvious ways in which you can promote the boss, one that might not come readily to mind, is to give him an early mention in the memos you write describing your ideas for improvement. You're going to get the major credit by dint of your authorship, so you can afford to share, to throw your boss a bone, a by-line. Whether he deserves the plug or not, start off your great-idea memos with "As a consequence of some conversations with my boss Mr. Big, I began looking into etc.," or "A chance remark of Mr. Big's started me thinking about etc." Be careful not to come on too gushy or heavy with "As a consequence of Mr. Big's inspiration and guidance, etc." That would be obsequious overkill and counterproductive to both of you. Such early mentions of your boss will incline him to relay your ideas on up. He will be disabused of any notions that you are trying to bypass him, that you are greedy, or that you represent a threat. He can't help responding gratefully to your sharing and shilling in this fashion, and will happily give your brainchildren his blessing and pass them along.

In communicating and relating to your boss, keep your eyes and ears open and utilize your objective approach by anticipating him and his problems. Initiative, simply translated, means doing things without being told. Don't wait for the boss to ask before doing something for him. Try to foresee his needs from the way matters are unfolding and developing, and get started on the necessary background homework. Be careful that you don't overdo. If you overstep your authority and tromp on the boss's toes and turf, he may rumble with you. Keep this kind of activity in the research area, the advance gathering of data that will be needed later. Don't prematurely, and without his consent, start any implementation or make any changes.

Suppose your boss says to you, "The last piece of the Smith jigsaw puzzle has finally fallen into place and we're going to have to hammer out some decisions and a course of action. How long do you think it will take to gather together all the background data we'll need in our considerations of what to do?" You may answer, "If I get started right away, turn all hands to, and burn the midnight oil, we ought to have all the information ready in four or five days." This is hardly what the boss hopes to hear. Instead, you should be able to say "I've been gathering what I thought we'd need as the Smith matter was developing. Now that the last piece of the puzzle is in place, I can have all the information in your hands right after lunch." Your boss will think you're great, and he'll be right. So try to anticipate what he's going to need, and try to get it ready for him before he asks for it.

To recapitulate: Communicate with and relate to your boss by accommodating to him and his needs. Make his job as easy for him as you can. Keep him continually informed by memo of the beginnings and ends of projects, and of changes in personnel, policy, and procedures. Provide him with optional solutions to the problems that arise, along with a recommendation. Go about your business with an upbeat, positive attitude. Confirm back to him in writing any verbal instructions he may give you, thus providing him with an opportunity to monitor against possible misunderstandings. Shill for your boss and try to promote him out of your way by touting him.

Try to anticipate what he will need and get started on it. Get to know what he is all about by compiling a profile, which will enable you to avoid becoming defensive about him and to accommodate to his idiosyncracies and subjectivity. Work with him, through him, and for him, not around him. Since he is the boss, give him his druthers. And never put him on the defensive, as he can retaliate in many ways, including firing you.

Practicing these precepts will make you invaluable. Your boss will want to keep you by his side. As he moves up the ladder with your help, he'll name you to succeed him, which is what you want and what it is all about.

HOW TO RELATE TO YOUR PEERS

As a manager moves upward into the higher echelons of the business he is in, the openings become fewer and the promotional opportunities narrower. And the competition becomes fiercer for those slots that are four, three, or two rungs down the ladder from the top. So beware of your peers and never trust them. They are your competitors and will do you in if you give them the chance. Don't make them your confidants. For they may use anything you may privately say, do, or even think about the job against you. Revelation and blackmail are frequently used to eliminate competitors in middle management or higher up. Don't leave yourself vulnerable by trusting peers and entrusting them with information that could be used to your career disadvantage. They may act buddy-

buddy, shaking your hand and smiling as they pat you on the back with the other hand. Don't put a knife in that other hand. You'll find yourself getting cut up and cut out. Rule number one in relating to your peers is never to trust them.

Rule number two is never to socialize with your peers. It's okay to take a coffee break or have lunch with them, or to have a quick drink at the station bar before catching your respective commuter trains. What we're talking about are the Friday night cocktail parties, the Saturday night dinner parties, the Sunday barbecues on somebody's patio—occasions when an entire peer group and their wives get together. Obviously, at such gatherings the major topic of conversation is going to be your mutual boss. Drinks and the presence of the wives are going to stimulate the natural competitiveness of the men and cause it to surface in one-upmanship games.

One peer might say, "You know something, guys. There are times lately when I'm beginning to think our mutual boss is getting to be a bit of an SOB." Whereupon a competing peer says, "What do you mean you're beginning to think he's an SOB? I came to that conclusion five years ago." Still another games-playing peer says, "You guys don't know what you're talking about. I reached that conclusion ten years ago, about two weeks after I came aboard." Another peer, not to be outdone, adds, "You guys aren't all that observant, saying he's only a bit of an SOB. In my book, he's been a big SOB for years." And someone else tops it with, "You guys are too generous. In my view, our boss was born an SOB."

54

All these men later realize they've said too much, and blackmail or worse is a distinct possibility. Their only recourse, to keep their comments from getting back to their boss, is to remove him. So they band together in self-defense with all the other members of the peer group and mount a campaign to get rid of the boss. Maybe they do and maybe they don't succeed. Either way, the situation is not good. They do not have a desirable work environment, conducive toward increased productivity and profitability, to say nothing of job satisfaction or even employee happiness. Studies show that much of the power politicking and many of the cliques and cabals so commonly encountered in business get started during such socializing by peer groups.

The only way to avoid dangerous involvement is to stay away from the places where so much of this kind of thing gets started. When you attend these gatherings, even if you exercise excellent restraint and refrain from joining the chorus of one-upmanship commentary, you're guilty by association. Besides, as an objective manager you have to maintain a neutral posture, not join sides or take a prejudiced stance. So, when you're invited to strictly peer group affairs, plead prior engagements.

You do not have to abstain totally from functions hosted by your peers. If you are invited to a wedding, graduation, or the like, you can cheerfully go as there is safety in the diversity of the guest list. Spend your time talking to the bride's mother, the minister, the cousin of the groom. Avoid congregating in some corner with your peers. Visit in moderation, making a point of not being among the last to leave. If you stay late you may get trapped into a peer group extension of the proceedings elsewhere with unfortunate results.

Refrain from joining company-sponsored bowling teams and the like. Too many members are not above taking advantage of the contact, using the camaraderie to gain special favors or to be forgiven for poor performance on the job. Avoid the problems. Prevent the unpleasantness of having someone from your team try to use you for his own ends.

Watch your behavior at affairs like the company picnic. Go, and do get into the softball game and sack races, etc. But after the sports are finished and it is getting dark, be careful. You obviously want to avoid your peers. You can't hobnob with your superiors; that would be highly visible bad form. Fraternizing with your troops, your subordinates, is also a no-no, for which you can be court-martialed. You can't prowl the areas where the wives are congregated or you'll be thought of as a questing tomcat. What can you safely do? Organize fun and games for the kids, and everyone will think you're great.

Be careful at the company golf outing. During the round everyone will be too busy coping with the course to politick or connive. After play has been completed and it is predinner cocktail time, take care. Don't sit down with any group, especially your peers. Imagine the thoughts that will go through any boss's mind when he sees all his subordinates gathered at a table, heads together, yakking among themselves. He'll think it's sedition, mutiny, revolt. Even a mixed group presents dangers. There's no way of telling how some higher-ups will interpret what's going on, innocent though it may be. Stay on your feet and circulate. Spend a few minutes here, say a few words there, and keep moving. Don't identify with any group by remaining with it beyond a few minutes or words. Under these circumstances you can visit briefly with both superiors and subordinates, safely asking how they played, congratulating low scorers, prize winners, or guys who have made eagles or holes in one.

If dinner seating is catch as catch can, try to pick a spot or table where there is a cross section or mix. If you can't don't worry. What with speeches, presentations of prizes, and all the other activities emanating from the head table, there won't be much opportunity for anything of a politicking nature to transpire, so you're safe. And go home early.

It is hardly necessary, I'm sure, to remind you to watch your drinking at any of these job-related social activities. Objective moderation is the order of the day. Any man who gets smashed on such occasions is very likely to have smashed his career as well.

Much of management today is conducted the democratic way, on a group basis, as a means of self-protection. If you are working for a sole proprietorship, the owner may very well run a one-man show. Professional managers do not like making unilateral decisions; it makes them both visible and vulnerable. As a survival tactic, decision making is dispersed over a group so that no one person shoulders 100 percent of the blame in case of mishap.

The onus is diluted by being shared. It is highly unlikely that ten men will be fired for a proportionate 10 percent of the blame, whereas if one person has 100 percent of the responsibility, he might be. By the same token, if the group decision is a winner, the man chairing the group is going to grab the credit. If the group decision is a bummer, he's going to say that all of the group opted to go this route, and all he did was rubber stamp and go along with their recommendation. It's all their fault, not his.

At any rate, management group meetings are usually held about once a week to hammer out courses of action and make decisions. An agenda is usually furnished. As a participant armed with the advance notice, do your homework and come up with your versions as to what needs to be done. You can't acquire visibility and credibility by hiding silently in the back seat of the last row at such meetings. Say your piece thoroughly and objectively, include the negatives as well as the positives, and see if you can't sell your idea. If you do succeed, as father to your brainchild you're going to be expected to go all out to see it work, to come to maturity.

Every now and then the majority of the group is not going to buy your idea, and will opt to go another way. Now you're in trouble, because you're identified with the losing position. Many managers do not realize their vulnerability in such cases. Maybe when the conference room door opens they refrain from showing their disappointment or disapproval. There are no storm clouds around their brows, no foot-dragging, no negatives apparent. Their appearance is one of upbeat, approving solidarity of purpose. But many subjective managers cannot go all out for things they don't believe in. They have to be convinced before they can put out and perform effectively. And this separates the men from the boys, the survivors from the nonsurvivors. In spite of lack of endorsement, lack of conviction, or lack of enthusiasm, for his own self-protection the manager identified with an opposition position must put out 110 percent to make the majority choice work.

Suppose he is right, and the way opted for by the majority doesn't work out. Inevitably a review meeting will be held by the group, a meeting that will resemble a wake. Hopefully, at this point our manager refrains from saying, "I told you so." Many subjective managers will happily see things go down the drain to prove their judgment. They couldn't care less about loss of time, money, image, or prestige on the part of the company. They'll sacrifice all these things to be proved right, which is objectively wrong. An objective manager in such an exposed and vulnerable position has to protect himself by working even harder to make something succeed that he doesn't believe in than he would for something he does believe in. Otherwise his peers will regard him as a handy fall guy on whom they can dump 100 percent of the blame, thereby absolving themselves from their 10 percent share.

Comes that wake, the guy chairing it might say, "Guys, we sure pulled a rock. Our idea never got off the pad at all, it never flew. Every man in this room worked hard to get it to fly with one exception. And that man

[you] opposed the idea from the very beginning and wanted to go another way. Had he done his share, had he cooperated, who knows, it might have flown." Thus your peers have handed you the empty bag, happily transferring the total blame to you, thereby absolving themselves of their proportionate share. You're visible, vulnerable, a handy fall guy, and you've been eliminated as a competitor for the narrowing openings above. In fact, you might wind up ticketed to go, and get your ticket punched.

You have to protect yourself by working so hard for the idea that when the wake comes, the man chairing it says, "Guys, we sure pulled a rock. Our idea never got off the pad at all, it never flew. Every man in this room worked hard to get it to fly, especially So-and-So [you], and he's the guy who told us right from the beginning that it would never fly. What we've learned from this disaster, men, is one thing. Next time, when So-and-So [you] says something isn't going to fly, maybe we all had better listen to him." You've gained credibility and visibility, and have removed yourself from the fall-guy category. You've protected yourself against your peers, who would happily do you in if you gave them the opportunity. Don't trust them, and don't give your competition the ammunition with which to shoot you down.

Just as you did with your boss, run a profile on your key competitors, the ones who are reporting to the same boss. Analyze their strengths and weaknesses so that you know what you're dealing with or competing against. Don't treat them as an entity or totality. That would be too much to tackle. Recognize that there are some things

60

you can't do anything about. Some of your competition may be bigger, handsomer, and more charming. Such assets you may not be able to overcome, so don't waste time trying.

Concentrate on how each man relates to and accommodates to your boss, how he communicates, how objective or subjective he is, to what degree he is neutral in his problem diagnoses, how thorough he is, how much he anticipates, how flexible he is. Try to match or exceed his strengths, and come down even harder in those areas in which you are strong and he is weak. As your competitor, he is one of your major problems. Diagnose what he is all about, and then prescribe and administer accordingly to overcome the problem. By breaking down his totality, you can effectively deal with manageable components of his overall makeup. Instead of throwing up your hands in defeat, saying, "He is what he is and I am what I am and there's no way I can compete," find chinks in his armor that will enable you to beat him.

To summarize: you don't want to make your peers defensive and retaliatory, so speak to them objectively and rephrase your messages. Use them as recipients of copies of your reports to your boss. Work with them, co-operate with them, to accomplish your mutual mission of making money, saving money, and solving problems to increase the profitability of your company. Don't trust them, however, and don't socialize with them. And just as they are trying to beat you to the slot above all of you, you've got to mount a campaign to beat them. Make a profile analysis of their strengths and weaknesses and an effort to match or excel the components making up their totalities. Never forget that your peers are your competition.

HOW TO COMMUNICATE WITH
AND RELATE TO SUBORDINATES

The first thing that needs to be done by any manager is to establish a chain of command — if one doesn't already exist. Pick out several key subordinates and make them your lieutenants. Have them pick out their sergeants, and have the sergeants designate their corporals. Stick with this chain of command by communicating only with your lieutenants; they in turn will pass the word down the line. Breaking this chain by dealing directly with those below your lieutenants or running troop information programs yourself will be bad for morale and performance. Nobody will be sure of his position, duties, and part in the structure. Instead of a chain, there'll be chaos.

Teach your lieutenants everything you know, including what you're learning from this book. Show them how to proceed objectively and how to sublimate their innate subjectivities. Let them know their mission is to accommodate to you, just as you are accommodating to your boss. Be sure they understand they are there to take care of you; you are not there to take care of them. Teach them how to avoid making people defensive and retaliatory. Require them to report regularly in writing on what they're doing. See to it that they provide options and alternative solutions, along with recommendations, on the problems facing your group. Make sure they confirm in writing, before implementation, any instructions you may give verbally, so that you can monitor for accuracy of understanding.

In other words, have your lieutenants do for you all the things we've suggested you do for your boss. Let them know that they will be getting copies of your upward communications so that they'll know exactly what you're doing and what's going on around them.

This kind of full disclosure is a tough hurdle to get over for many insecure or otherwise subjective managers. They prefer to withhold, to maintain a distance from their subordinates, whom they blanketly regard as threats to their security. They don't even want to share, never mind give away the store. Such managers are not trying to build empire. They are preserving empire, unaware that they thereby abort their upward mobility potentials.

For example, a new job opens up. Top management is evaluating which of two in-house managers to fill it with. One candidate is a timid empire preserver. He has greater seniority and more experience. If they tap him for the promotion, however, things in his current area of operation will come to a screeching halt because he has not trained anyone to succeed him. The other candidate is less senior, less qualified, and less experienced. But he does have several trained understudies ready to step into his shoes and role. If he is chosen, his current end of the operation will continue as smoothly as before, without a hitch or downtime.

The choice becomes obvious to top management. It has the objective overview, not a subjective, narrow concern about who deserves the promotion on the basis of seniority. Naturally, the bypassed senior manager is going to grumble about politics and say that the junior man was picked because he buttered up the top brass. He is wrong, of course, but he is bound to rationalize and blame everybody else for his misfortune, never realizing that he dug his own grave.

Don't be timid of, and protective about, your present position. If you are you don't belong in your present job, or even deserve it. A good objective manager conducts himself daily with the thought in mind that on his way home tonight he may step off a curb and be run over. He has a fiduciary responsibility to his company to provide for his successor, to see that the wheels he is responsible for keep turning.

So have the guts and objectivity to groom your lieutenants to succeed you. If you don't have somebody ready to take over, you're not apt to be promoted. In fact, you may not even be successful in preserving your empire, as top management won't want to depend that much on one person — someone who might become incapacitated or leave. It would prefer a cushion, a reserve, a safety factor. Sooner or later the manager who holds back will be replaced by someone who will teach, train, and make full disclosure to his understudies.

See to it that your lieutenants communicate with and

train their sergeants, the sergeants their corporals, and so on down the chain of command. It may be impractical and unrealistic for all your corporals to carry Napoleonic marshal's batons in their knapsacks. But you do want them trained your way, aware of your objectives and how you propose to attain them. You want your entire command cooperating and communicating on the wavelengths you've established.

You'll be running a very effective job-enrichment program for your charges in that they'll know what is going on and what their part in it is. Lack of information as to goals and lack of a feeling of involvement are two of the most common complaints voiced by unhappy employees. By filling in these communications voids you'll be captaining a tight ship, but a happy one. Your crew will give you maximum performance in full and cheerful awareness of what you expect of them in order to accomplish your mutual mission.

One of the areas in which a manager's lack of objectivity shows up badly is his handling of new employees. Because he likes a trainee, or feels sorry for him, he frequently will keep him on long past the end of the usual training term in the hope of bringing him up to minimum performance standards. This is a waste of the firm's money. If a manager makes a habit of this he'll eventually have nothing but minimum performers on hand, with the total effectiveness of his operation downgraded. He does not realize that his subjective approach, his emotion of friendship or sympathy, is making him and the area he is managing look bad. He'd be better advised to get rid of minimal performers. Their replacements might turn out to be whizzes who will upgrade the overall level of performance in the operation.

An objective manager would go to his boss the pay period before the end of the training term and say, "Trainee Jones isn't going to make it, even to minimum standard. His spelling and grammar aren't that good, and the words just don't flow freely and fast enough. He's miscast in the role of sales correspondent. But I've discovered he has a flair for figures and is very good at detail and organizing. We could let him go, or we could retain our investment in him and come up with a very effective performer by transferring him to market research. I recommend the transfer, but what do you think, boss?" Whichever alternative the boss opts for is now confirmed in writing. "On such and such a date what to do about trainee Jones was discussed. The options were to let him go or to transfer him to market research. The decision was to transfer him."

Another area in which subjectivity shows up often and is a big disadvantage is in regard to the long-time employee who can no longer perform satisfactorily. This is the old Joe Blow type who has spent forty good years on the line but is now coming up with too much rework and spoilage because he's lost his hand and eye coordination. Obviously, something needs to be done about him, but Joe Blow's boss feels sorry for him and does nothing. He rationalizes that if he lets Joe go morale of Joe's associates will suffer and he'll be thought a callous brute. He wants to continue being regarded as a "good boss" and not lose his popularity among his subordinates, Joe's peers. He further rationalizes that Joe is only costing them $15,000 a year all told with fringes, and the company will never miss that, can easily afford it. So he keeps Joe on the line for a few more years until he can retire.

Because of his rigid, unilateral, subjective approach it never occurs to this manager that other and better options are available. He is also inviting intercession from his boss, which is deadly. One of the worst things that can happen to any manager is to have his boss come to him and tell him to get rid of one of his subordinates. It says that that manager's boss deems him incapable of an adequate overview. That manager is no longer going anywhere, except maybe out. In fact, he might be well advised to start looking for fresh track on which to run, as he has derailed his career train where he is now.

An objective manager would be aware that today Joe Blow is in a different position from the one he would have been in forty years ago. Had he been let go then when he was sixty years old, there would have been few options. It would have meant the end of the line—the breadline or the end of the dock. But today, what with separations settlements, unemployment insurance, rehabilitation training, social security, and other programs, Joe Blow isn't that badly off. The same manager would realize that he is running one of forty departments, each of which has one or two Joe Blows aboard. And there are six companies of forty departments each making up the corporation. Fifteen thousand dollars times an average of one and a half Joe Blows times forty departments times six companies equals more than a $5.4 million loss, an amount that could represent the difference between a good year and a bad year, a year in the black and a year in the red. It might even represent the difference between staying in business and folding.

There is mutual fiduciary responsibility in management, and a dependence on fellow managers to do their duty, to do what is required of them to keep the ship afloat. An analogy: Suppose a newly commissioned ensign in the navy draws his first sea duty as damage-control officer for a compartment below the waterline of a carrier or cruiser. Our ensign is ambitious, politically aware, and careful, and aspires to make it topside and eventually to the bridge. His ship gets involved in an action with an enemy and sustains some hits, some damage. Our ensign discovers he has a couple of leaks in his compartment. A subjective approach makes him afraid to take positive action for fear he'll be judged by his superiors to have overreacted, to have hit the panic button without due cause. He's afraid action on his part will impede his progress to the bridge. He rationalizes that the leak flow is not that great, that the pumps will take care of it. He abdicates his fiduciary responsibility to the group and refrains from doing what has to be done because of his subjective concern for his image.

If all damage-control officers aboard thought the same way and refrained from plugging the leaks in their compartments, the whole ship would founder in one hell of a hurry, and nobody would make it to the bridge; they wouldn't even make it topside. In the navy, stormy seas and danger to the vessel mean the officers on the bridge will concern themselves primarily with keeping the ship afloat. They'll do anything required to accomplish this, even jettison cargo—including multimillion-dollar fighter planes—and crew. They can always get more cargo and fighter planes and train more crew. The unforgivable thing, the one act that would ruin their careers, would be to lose the ship. They'd never get another command.

Business is no different from the military in this regard. Managers must plug the leaks in their compartments or departments to keep the operation afloat. All their fellow managers are depending on them to perform this mutual fiduciary duty. Otherwise, everyone may find himself in the same sinking boat and they may all perish together because of the derelictions of a few unaware and subjective crew members.

So a manager cannot procrastinate or drag his feet when confronted with a Joe Blow. He must go to his boss promptly when the problem becomes apparent, saying, "Our most senior man on the line, Joe Blow, can't hack it anymore. He's got the shakes, and is killing us with rework and spoilage. I've talked to him about staying on as third broom in the maintenance department for a couple of years until he can retire. He's willing to take the demotion and transfer, rather than be let go. But, there's a third option, boss. Joe's been on that line longer and knows it better than anybody else around. True, he's lost his hand and eye coordination, but there's nothing wrong with his eyes, only his hands. I think we could keep him on until retirement, and get a lot more good mileage out of him by transferring him to Quality Control and making him an inspector on that line he knows so well. Instead of firing or demoting him we'd be promoting him. I'm in favor of making him an inspector. What do you think, boss?"

After the boss has agreed to the recommendation or has chosen one of the other options, the manager confirms in writing that on that date three alternatives had been considered for Joe Blow, and he will make the final decision.

A manager who has taught the objective overview to his lieutenants and had them teach it to their sergeants on down the line, would not have morale problems among Joe Blow's peers unless he did nothing about him. Everyone in the operation, right down to the lowest line level, would understand that some disposition has to be made of problem people. If they saw that management's policy was to take the easy way out by sweeping Joe Blows under rugs, they'd start to worry about the safety of their own jobs and the security and long-range potential of the entire company and operation.

Even the lowliest underlings could be made aware of what is going on from the standpoint of top management, and learn to take the global, overview approach. This is not an impossible dream. A utopian business climate can be achieved quite easily if you utilize the precepts you have been learning here and share your managerial phi-

70

losophy with your subordinates. This philosophy is management by objective, objectively arrived at through options and alternatives.

RELATING TO THE OUTSIDE WORLD

Customers

Now you know how to communicate with and relate to your bosses, your peers, and your subordinates, who make up the bulk of your work environment. But there are other components in the picture, such as customers, suppliers, and competitors. As for customers, remember, always be a house man first. It is easier to find a new customer than a new house. Identify objectively with your company. Don't try to curry favor and be a customer's man by siding with and relating to the customer every time there is a problem between your company and that customer. Don't blame the factory or the shipping department for nondelivery of goods. That is only subjective tea and sympathy. If you can't deliver, come up with an objective reason for nonperformance.

You represent your company, the totality of its parts, so front for it, defend it, and don't blame or malign it or any aspect of it. Bad-mouthing your company is no way to earn respect for it or for yourself. You and your company could very well lose a customer permanently that way.

In your contacts with prospects be sure to talk about them, their needs, and the long-term benefits they will derive from doing business with your company. Leave yourself and what you hope to gain completely out of the picture. They couldn't care less that you need the business to make your quota or a bonus. As you relate to prospects, don't come on transiently or in that much of a hurry to make a sale. In other words, don't concentrate on making individual sales, applying pressure to bring about a quick close. Instead, decompress the buyer–seller relationships by neither rushing nor pushing prospects.

The image you should project is that of trying to build lasting relationships with customers in the full knowledge that they will take care of your sales for you. Show them that you expect to continue to enjoy their accounts and business because of your follow-up, follow-through, and objective, thorough service. You will handle their business as a good house man for a good house, not as a servile, fawning customer's man. Your prospects undoubtedly have customers, too; don't behave in any way they wouldn't want their own front people to behave.

Suppliers

Don't be arbitrary and unreasonably demanding with suppliers just because you have the clout, are in the driver's seat, and can call the shots. Let the other guy live too, and even make a buck. Otherwise you might just kill off a hard-to-replace source. Recognize that now and then there will be a lack of coordination, a late delivery, or even a mistake, just as happens with your company, so don't be an overly punitive hell raiser. Do unto the other guy what you would like from him if your positions were reversed. Don't expect to be overly entertained, just as you don't expect to overentertain your customers. We covered socializing earlier when we counseled objective moderation in any job-related social activity. In summary, don't exact any more tribute from your suppliers than you are prepared to pay your customers.

Competitors

As for communicating with and relating to competitors, don't get cute and excessively sharp with them to the extent that your ethics can be questioned. Don't rap them. Such an act could backfire to your discomfiture to the point where you may be fired, or even to the filing of a libel suit. If your competition uses gutter tactics, you don't have to descend to its level and roll around with it in the mud. You might close a deal, one you wouldn't have made otherwise, going that route. But what about the cost? You probably did not make a lasting customer, and what about the name and reputation of your company, and you? The whole mess might wind up with you and your company very much the net losers when you close a deal by subterfuge or other ethically questionable tactics.

For everyone's sake, your company's and yours, win on merit, not by playing the angles better than your competitors. You don't build customers or a career by having a reputation in the industry of being a blue-suede-shoe quick-buck artist who creams the marketplace. If you do, you can never go back, you've always got to keep creaming. After a while you run out of marketplace, there's no place left to go, and you'll get thrown out if you try to cover the same ground again.

That road is not the one to take to promote your long-range career. There's room out there both for you and your company and for your competition. Don't be greedy, trying to get all the business by destroying your competitors by foul means if necessary. Try to get a bigger share of the market fairly. Treat your competitors as a potential resource for your upward mobility aspirations. Don't do anything that might spoil a possible career with them if anything happens where you are. They are your most logical and nearest transfer points.

If you have to resituate, the greater the radius of career transfer, the more difficult it becomes, and the greater the discount in earnings will be. A company must make a profit on what everyone in its employ does, from the porter to the president. The faster your actions make a profit for a new employer, the better for you. He might be willing to invest in you, but he will not indulge you. The longer he thinks it will take you to adjust your skills and experience to your environment and make a profit for him, the less he will pay you to begin with. So protect yourself and your earnings by treating your competition as potential future employers. Going to the competition constitutes the shortest radius of transfer if you have to move. Don't do anything to endanger this resource, this career insurance, by irresponsible behavior toward or about your competitors.

The last thing you need to concern yourself about in the area of communications and relating is yourself.

You've learned the do's and don'ts. You've learned to proceed in objective, rather than subjective, fashion. As a consequence, you are not performing in a vacuum. Your excuses are gone; you now know better. You understand what is expected of you.

All of us fear the unknown. Once it becomes known, we no longer fear it as much, and our self-confidence grows. It takes guts and effort to sublimate our innate subjectivity and to proceed objectively, especially when we may feel ourselves to be largely alone in such an approach, when we perceive our work associates as practicing members of the great subjective majority in business management. Have confidence and courage in doing what you know is right, even if you are outnumbered. If you do, you're bound to survive and prosper in management. Good luck!

PART II

Self-Marketing

Many readers will retrieve stagnant or even deteriorating careers by practicing the precepts they have learned so far. Other readers will recognize that they are in an incompatible work environment because of their makeups and psychologies, and that a change of scene is not only desirable but necessary. This is the primary target of this section, and should help these readers in making a career change with maximum effectiveness.

The dynamics of the marketplace may also unexpectedly force content people from apparently secure and satisfactory career slots. The material covered in this section may serve as form of insurance against such an unhappy eventuality. Awareness and utilization of what is yet to come may forestall or prevent many forced separations. Should the fall of the ax be inevitable, the reader will be able to quickly mount an effective self-marketing campaign. That campaign should result in a group of career-resuming offers to evaluate.

At the very least, even if no voluntary or involuntary change takes place, the balance of this book can be a learning tool for anyone involved in interviewing and hiring, or firing, subordinates. The principles that follow are equally applicable from either side of the interview desk.

Setting Up the Interview

PURPOSE

The average uninformed interviewee is convinced that the interview is an examination of his competence. So he concentrates on this aspect, coming on hard and heavy regarding his technological expertise. Any time the conversation departs from the matter of competence, he gets nervous and tries to bring it back to how well he can do this job, standing on his head with one hand tied behind his back. In return he hopes to hear the right set of numbers regarding compensation and thinks that he then has a deal. Unfortunately for him, this attitude is far removed from reality.

In the usual interview situation, a slate of candidates has somehow been arrived at from among perhaps hundreds of applicants. Résumés have been carefully screened, and inquiries have been made of previous employers. The prospective employer is satisfied that the half-dozen or so applicants remaining for interview are in the ball park with regard to competence.

What he is checking on in the interview is another factor, and the most important one in the equation — the matter of compatibility. He already has a pretty good idea of the candidate's professionalism. What he now wants to know is what kind of person the prospective employee is. How does he conduct himself while on the job? Will he fit into the team? Will he get along with his associates? Will he blend into the environment, chemistry, and climate? Will he be able to implement the company's policy? In other words, will he be of help with the problems, or will he be a problem himself? That's what the interview is all about — compatibility.

Management status has been attained through a discipline, such as engineering or accounting. But somewhere in the process of upward mobility a point was reached at which that manager had to turn his back on his discipline. He was no longer handling problems in his field. Instead he was managing people, and people problems, and problem people, who were handling the problems in his field for him. He was in an entirely different ball game. You can't engineer people with a slide-rule approach, nor do they infallibly add up like an accountant's column of figures. Instead, a manager must plan, motivate, and coordinate the efforts of his people. The skills needed to accomplish this successfully are quite different from technological expertise. They are predicated entirely on objectivity.

A subjective manager will only be able to relate to, and communicate with, the people who are on his precise wavelength. Obviously, those who take the identical stance, who see eye to eye with him on everything, are going to be relatively few. His subjective approach is going to conflict with the subjectivities of his associates, and he will wind up constantly butting heads with the great majority of the people around him who are not on his exact wavelength. In other words, in no way is he going to be successful at managing people even though he may be a great technician. His prejudices, stance, and convictions may position him completely out of the gray, middle area of objectivity alluded to earlier—he is in the black or white area. Thus, he cannot relate to or even reach the people whose subjectivity places them at a diametrically opposed position.

To have any chance of relating and communicating, a manager must not operate from black or white extreme positions, but from the middle gray area of objectivity. He can then reach the people at both ends, and have some chance of bringing them back to the gray, desirable area. He will never convert people who feel that white is superior to the black position, or vice versa. The distance and stretch are too great. He would be accomplishing little anyway; one subjective extreme would simply be exchanged for another.

People proceeding from different positions of subjective bias and conviction must inevitably clash. But it takes two to tangle. If a subjective person encounters an objective one, there will be no conflict. The subjective person may be ready to fight, to punch, but there is no target, no antagonist, if the other person remains objective. So the potential confrontation is controlled and never comes off, thanks to objectivity. In other words, an objective manager operating in the gray middle area can reach, and relate to, anyone. There are no personality clashes, no philosophic differences, no problems arising from two subjective personalities butting heads.

The knowledgeable interviewer or prospective employer is probing for evidences of objectivity in the interviewee. He can't find anything out from discussions about the technology, the discipline. An engineer can be quite objective about his engineering, an accountant about his accounting. To determine how objective the prospect will be with people he'll be managing, the interviewer will have to talk about people topics — current events, politics, sports, national figures and affairs, and so forth — topics that are of general interest and concern to all people regardless of what they may do for a living. These are the make-or-break questions in the interview, the ones from which hiring evaluations and decisions will be made.

Unfortunately, most people being interviewed aren't aware of what's going on, and how important it is. They regard these questions as a deviation from the interview. They interpret such public domain questions as a coming up for air, a breather, a conversational recess or break. So they pay little attention, give short answers, and impatiently try to bring the conversation back to the matter of competence. They're talking apples to the interviewer's oranges, and doing themselves a disservice by displaying subjectivity and an unawareness of the purpose of the questions. In short, they're flunking the interview. They are not displaying the objectivity the interviewer is hoping to find. He already has too many naive and subjective managers on hand and certainly doesn't need more of the same.

CLIMATE

Another common error made by unknowing interviewees is to assume that the interview begins only when they are in the office of Mr. Big, the man with whom they have their appointment. That would be the case when Mr. Big is the owner of a sole proprietorship, running a one-man show. Otherwise Mr. Big is far more likely to be an employee, a professional manager. If he makes solo decisions and makes a mistake in hiring, he is visible and vulnerable, with the person he brought in constantly around reminding everyone of Mr. Big's bad judgment. So, in self-defense and to protect himself and his position, Mr. Big is going to invoke consultative help from his associates when making hiring decisions, just as he holds regular management meetings to deal with operational problems.

If a group decision has been made to hire someone who turns out badly, Mr. Big can say, "All you people thought he was great, so I went along with the consensus even though I had some reservations about him." In this way Mr. Big has absolved himself from blame, transferring it to the group. On the other hand, should the new employee really prove to be great, Mr. Big will be quick to grab all the credit, saying, "He's my boy. I hired him." At any rate, many people will be involved in a hiring decision, some of them most unlikely participants in the opinion of the unaware interviewee. In other words, the interviewing process starts as soon as the interviewee is within sight or hearing distance of *anybody* in the employ of that company. And the same applies on the way out. The interview does not end when the candidate leaves Mr. Big's office.

For illustrative purposes let's construct a hypothetical interview situation. We will load it with the ultimate in deviousness to prepare you for the worst that could happen. In all probability most of your interviews will be less tricky, for which you should count your blessings. But you might be unlucky and run into some highly sophisticated interviews, wherein traps are being set for your unwary foot every step of the way. If you are aware and prepared to cope with these successfully, the less sophisticated ones will be that much easier.

So, we have an unaware and subjective manager named Smith who flies to a distant city for an interview with Mr. Big. He is met at the airport by a young man driving a company car. Smith dismisses this man as nothing but a chauffeur whose only function is to drive him to the plant premises. This subjective prejudgment is a mistake. The man is the whizz kid of the personnel department, with a master's degree in psychology. He is a very important member of the group making the hiring decision. His job is to start evaluating Smith and his objectivity, to determine his compatibility and potential for success as a manager.

Some conversation is required. A logical place to start is for the chauffeur to ask, "How was your flight in, Mr. Smith?" Back comes a careless, unaware reply: "We sat in the plane at the airport for an hour and a half while the ground crew fiddled around with the hydraulic system. It was miserable because the air conditioning had to be off, so we all sweltered. Then, there wasn't a damn magazine on the plane I hadn't already read, so I just sat twiddling my thumbs. When they got things fixed we wound up the twenty-seventh plane in the taxi line. By the time we finally took off, the steaks were cold and the martinis warm. When we arrived here, weather had us stacked up for a couple of hours before we could land. So, it was a bad flight from start to finish, and for my dough, you can give aviation back to the Wright Brothers."

By now you should recognize how wrong but natural this answer was, and why the chauffeur would give it a big black mark. Smith should have brought along his own reading and writing materials in anticipation of delay. He showed no neutrality of approach, and high bias instead. He was not flexible. During the hour and a half wait the stewardess surely would have let him off to buy fresh reading material. Barring that, if he had asked, the passenger service representative would have brought unread magazines or papers to him. He also demonstrated a very negative attitude throughout.

Furthermore, he demonstrated that he is pressure

prone, and pressure is a cumulative thing. These days it isn't just the marketing and sales people who travel a lot. Everybody travels to some degree. Smith might have the misfortune to run into three or four bad flights back to back with pressure accumulating to the breaking point. He might arrive somewhere, have someone trigger him with a wrong word, and blow his cork. There goes a client, contract, or potential customer.

All in all, he showed no objectivity, a high degree of subjectivity, an undesirable attitude, and a susceptibility to pressure. He flunked chauffeur badly, and it is unlikely that anything he might do or say later will be sufficient to overcome this first bad impression. The probability is that he will only confirm or worsen this initial negative response which he so innocently and naively generated.

What Smith should have said to the chauffeur is, "O'Hare is a pretty busy place and you have to expect a lack of coordination once in a while. Well, today we had one. But during the delay before takeoff, I had a chance to catch up on some required reading I'd brought along. In fact, I even had time to write an overdue letter to my mother. I'm awfully sorry you had to wait around for three and a half hours. What did you do with yourself? There doesn't seem to be much around in the way of amusement."

This response would demonstrate objectivity — anticipation, flexibility, thoroughness. It would exhibit the ability to convert negatives to positives, which is what management is all about — the solving of problems consists of converting negatives into positives. Also, Smith was demonstrating interpersonal skill, an ability to handle people, by inquiring about the chauffeur's activities during the delay. He recognized that the waiting period could have been an annoying or even a trying experience for the driver, who might have a pile of paper or pressing matters or both back on his desk clamoring for attention, and that he might have to work overtime to catch up for the lost three and a half hours. The man could also have a dinner date or other appointment for that night that he might have to cancel because of Smith.

Smith's concern for the chauffeur will go a long way toward nullifying any antipathy that might have built up because of the delay. The man knows that it is not Smith's fault he is late. But he has still been inconvenienced by the delay, and nobody can possibly be 100 percent objective. There is bound to be some resentment despite master's degrees in psychology. Smith's answer would have gotten everything back on an objective basis. Smith would get a high passing mark from the chauffeur, and would create a very strong initial impression that would not erode a great deal if he should slip a bit as the conversation continues during the drive. The chauffeur will not discuss Smith's work. He'll talk about sports, current events, politics, or names, places, and faces in the news.

He might ask next, "Mr. Smith, you're from Chicago, and I've got a question. What happened to your Cubs the last few years? They were loaded with talent and looked like sure pennant winners, but got nowhere." Smith would probably come up with a subjective answer, blaming leftovers from Durocher, or Lockman, Marshall, or Wrigley. An objective man is a good team man, and does not select individuals for blame. He will blame systems, overall functions, generic things instead. An objective manager is supposed to be alert, aware, informed, but not partisan — not that much of a "fan." The word fan is an abbreviated form of the word fanatic, which is an emotional, unreasoning example of extreme subjectivity. If Smith didn't have an answer he'd have been better off saying, "I don't know" rather than come on in partisan fashion.

Hopefully Smith would reply cerebrally, logically, intellectually, and objectively as follows: "You're right. The Cubs were loaded with talent. But the major league pension system pays a player $15,000 a year for life starting at the age of fifty-five after they have put in ten years in the majors. Too many of the Cubs were reaching their eighth, ninth, and tenth years of tenure simultaneously. From current life expectancy charts the money to be collected consistently from the pension represented a lot more than a share of winning a single pennant. So everyone was careful not to get hurt. With only another year or so to go toward pension vestment, nobody wanted to be injured and sent down to the minors at the eleventh hour.

"Wrigley Field became not so much an arena as a theater. Players were going through the motions, their lines, acting out their parts in safety. You didn't see diving catches, guys crashing off walls, and the like. Everyone was afraid of getting hurt, getting sent down and thereby losing their pensions. Withholding their best effort caused them to lose an awful lot of ball games they could have won. The Cubs established all kinds of records for losing ball games by one run, games that could have been won by extra effort that was not forthcoming because of the pension system. My view is not generally shared by most Chicagoans, but that's what I think happened to the Cubs."

This objective reply would get a high passing mark from the chauffeur. But having a job to do he would probably persist, answering, "That analysis of the Cub situation sounds very logical and reasonable, and I'm glad to have had the benefit of your insight. Along the same lines, whatever happened to your Bears?"

In all probability, Mr. Smith would blame Halas, Gibron, Dooley, Douglas, or Finks. Take your choice of any one, any combination, or all together. And if he did not follow pro football it would never occur to Smith to admit it. Instead, he'd manufacture some mishmash, totally unaware that he was hammering another nail in his own coffin.

Had he been objective and aware, Smith would have said, "A lot of our well-meaning, loyal Chicago sports-writers blew a lot of journeyman players up to star proportions because they wished the Bears well. Besides, they had to justify their own existence and got carried away by their own rhetoric. Also, it was the only and oldest game in town. Once a season began it didn't take long for reality to assert itself by way of the competition. Of the twenty-six teams playing pro football the Bears have one of the lowest payrolls, and I've learned in life that you only get what you pay for. Not that you can blame Halas. He's one of the founders of pro football and dates back to the days when he himself only got fifty bucks a game. So it is understandable that he would be reluctant to give multimillion-dollar no-cut contracts to untried collegians even if they did make All-American. Too many of them have never made it in the pros, and too many All-Pros were nobodies coming from obscure colleges.

"Halas is going with the percentages and trying to find and develop the sleepers. They greatly outnumber the name stars who made it after college anyway. So far he hasn't been that lucky or successful. He's found a few key guys but not enough to put together a contender. But in time he probably will, or so all of Chicago hopes. At any rate, that's my view of the Bear situation, Mr. Chauffeur."

Again, this objective answer has to score high in the chauffeur's evaluation of Smith, his compatibility and his people-handling capability. For the duration of the drive from the airport to the plant the conversation would continue in this vein. The thing to remember is that it is not just random, aimless talk, a conversational filling in of awkward travel time. There is a purpose behind it. The interview has started, whether Smith knows it or not!

Now let's make a bit of a switch. We'll continue with interviewee Smith, but this time the interview is closer and he drives to his appointment. Traffic is terrible. He arrives a half hour late and is consequently disturbed and concerned. When he reaches the reception room he finds the receptionist is a gorgeous, sexy female. Smith jumps to the conclusion that she is too ornamental to be competent. His masculinity is titillated by her femininity and he wants to make a good impression on her as a man, not necessarily as a candidate for a managerial position.

It never occurs to Smith that the receptionist might be a plant, there for his benefit or detriment as the case may be. She too could be out of personnel with a master's in psychology. Her mission is to make early evaluations of Smith. She begins by asking him "How was the drive over, Mr. Smith?" Mr. Smith comes up with a personality-guy answer of humorous intent: "Everybody in the world who has wheels was out on them today, and it was bumper to bumper all the way with all the idiots trying to kill each other. It was a real hair-raiser getting here and that's why I'm late. This guy Nader has the right idea but he doesn't take it far enough. Never mind seat belts, shoulder harnesses, air bags, and all that nonsense. What we need in next year's models are straitjackets for the drivers."

The receptionist may dutifully and politely respond with a ha-ha, but in the meantime she's giving him a flunking mark because of his highly subjective answer. He has exhibited none of the components of objectivity. He has displayed a negative attitude and approach, and revealed himself to be pressure prone. And his attempt at humor, neither called for nor appropriate, might be interpreted by her as smacking of male chauvinism, a very early verbal pass, or an indication that he is a potential tomcat not safe to be let loose among the women in the company.

Smith should have said, "What with all the bad weather we've had lately there were an awful lot of people out driving today playing catch-up on errands that had accumulated for over a week. So it was pretty trafficky all the way. But when I woke up this morning and saw the sun shining for a change I knew that would happen. I started out a half hour earlier to get here on time. The drive over was most interesting; I'd never driven so far in this direction before. I listened on the car radio to several fine talk shows from local stations en route, and I even heard all four movements of one of my favorite symphonies."

This answer gets a high mark. It shows anticipation, flexibility, a positive attitude, no vulnerability to pressure, and a neutral and neuter approach to her femininity. The receptionist cannot fault his reply. She will proceed to seat him, hang up his hat and coat, and offer him coffee. And she will hand him a newspaper she has previously read carefully, noting which section he reads. Whether it is sports, editorial, stock quotations, or even the comic section — perish forbid! — she will be prepared to talk with him about it. The topics will be general and impersonal, but they will enable her to evaluate his objectivity, compatibility, and skill with people. While Smith is settling into reading the paper she'll be making notes about his appearance, his clothes, etc. Is he sitting on the edge of the seat, ill at ease, mopping his brow, biting his nails? Or does he seem calm, cool, and poised?

The receptionist notes that Smith is reading the first page, so she says "I see our friend Nixon has made the headlines again. Gone but not forgotten! What do you think of him, Mr. Smith?" She is not interested in Smith's politics or the content of his answer. Her concern is how he answers. Smith might say, "I think he was the victim of the liberal Eastern Establishment. After he made them look like fools by winning with such a huge plurality, they resolved to lynch him and succeeded. He should still be in office as the greatest president of modern times, and they should be carving him up on Mount Rushmore and minting coins showing his profile."

Such an answer would flunk because it shows rigid and inflexible conviction, prejudice, and bias. It is highly subjective, and certainly does not come from the gray, neutral area of objectivity. The same would pertain if Smith had answered from the opposite extreme, saying, "I'll never forgive Ford for having given him a pardon. They ought to bury the bum up to his neck in sand somewhere out on Big Sur and let the ants and the gulls and the crabs finish him off."

A highly passing objective response would have been, "Nixon sure had a hard time of it and I certainly don't envy him. While he was president he seemed to be making his judgments from about as complete and accurate information as it was possible to gather. It may even have been somewhat overdone, as in Watergate. But what I know about such matters is so second-hand and fragmented, I don't feel I'm in a position to second-guess him. There is still too much emotionality intruding into the

93

Nixon matter. Until all the muss, fuss, and dust have quieted down it will be hard to evaluate him objectively. Such an evaluation might not even be possible for this generation. We may have to leave it to future historians who will be able to bring more perspective and objectivity to the evaluation process than we can right now."

The receptionist might then go on to other items appearing in the first section of the paper, saying "NASA is back in the news after a pretty long absence. What do you think about the space program, Mr. Smith?" His reply might very well be, "It's the boondoggle of the ages. We taxpayers have been ripped off for billions of dollars that could have been spent on health, education, and welfare, and all we have to show for it is that we now know the moon isn't made of green cheese." Such a subjective answer would be wrong.

Smith might have gone to the opposite extreme, saying, "It's the greatest achievement of humanity, and it's too bad they cut back the budget. If we are to survive as a species, someday we'll probably have to colonize out there in space after we've exhausted our terrestrial resources." The response would still be wrong.

An objective answer would have been, "There seem to be two popular schools of thought on the space matter. One is that it is the green cheese boondoggle, and the other that it is the greatest, and humanity's ultimate salvation. A third group of much fewer people think it was a political power ploy prompted by our competitive rivalry with the Russians. I think it is too early to make a judgment because all the returns aren't in yet. There were all kinds of scientific breakthroughs in the way of space medicine, exotic alloys, adhesives, and miniaturization. The research and engineering have been done. It's now only a matter of reducing costs to make some of these things commercially feasible. Before too much longer we taxpayers are going to be enjoying all kinds of fallout benefit from the billions we've spent on space. Until we know what these are, we can't make an objective evaluation of the space program and its worth."

At this point another planted participant in the interview evaluation may appear on the scene from out back somewhere, perhaps on signal from the receptionist. He introduces himself to Mr. Smith as Mr. Medium, saying, "As I was passing Mr. Big's office he called me in and asked me to tell you he's tied up on a long-distance conference call straightening out some problem. He's apt to be another twenty minutes to a half hour so he asked me to keep you company. I hear you're from Chicago. How would you feel about leaving it and relocating here if you're hired? Would you miss it?"

Smith might hasten to say that he wouldn't miss it at all, that it is a terrible place to live, that the weather is awful, that the crime rate has risen out of sight, and so on. In his effort to come on favorably for resituating he has overdone it. He has rapped and bum-rapped Chicago, displaying subjective bias and prejudice and a lack of objectivity — the quality that is being looked for by Mr. Medium and all the others involved in the group interview. He may have honestly conveyed his true feelings about Chicago, but in so doing he flunked. An objective manager would have sublimated his subjectivity and stayed in the gray, median area.

A better, realistic, and passing reply would have been, "Any time a family relocates there are going to be a few initial hurdles to get over. Friends, activities, and familiar neighborhoods are bound to be missed, if only out of habit. Getting resettled and picking up new friends and activities always takes time. But our family is quite gregarious and extroverted, and we've been through relocations before. There may be fewer activities here than in Chicago because this is a smaller city. But that is an advantage because it will enable us to get involved in more of the things that go on. So we're looking forward to the change."

Mr. Medium might then get into a discussion of the various kinds of activities available, to get some idea of Smith's major interests. Or he might change topics completely to something else, such as "What are your hobbies?" or "What do you do with your spare time?" or "What are your sports?" If Smith comes on as a buff or aficionado of anything by replying, "I spend every minute I can on the golf course," "I put in a lot of hours on my stamp collection," or "I go fishing at every opportunity," it will be taken by Mr. Medium as an indication of lopsided interest that perhaps approaches compulsive extremes or even neurosis.

Smith would score better with Mr. Medium by telling him he's interested in a lot of things and does them in moderation. He bowls, golfs, fishes, and plays tennis, handball, and squash. This would show a broad, rounded development rather than a specialized concentration to the point of phobia on any one thing. Remember that Mr. Medium most probably isn't trying to find a fellow golf nut. He's checking out Smith's objectivity.

Other passers-by may join in the conversation between Smith and Mr. Medium, and perhaps ask a people question or two of Smith, who assumes that they just accidently wandered by and are being sociable and neighborly. Unfortunately for him, they are part of the evaluating team, and are coming by perceptions about Smith and his objectivity, or lack of it, from his unwary replies and comments.

At any rate, what Smith views as merely a coffee klatch finally breaks up, and Smith is shown into the office of Mr. Big, the man with whom his appointment is set up. Mr. Big gives Smith about five minutes of courteous conversation about the weather and Smith is out. The interview is over. Smith goes home in bewilderment and tells his friends and family, "That sure is an idiot company. They went to all the trouble and expense of bringing me in and all I got from Mr. Big was a fast five minutes and out. I never had a chance to tell him how well I could do the job. I spent more time talking a lot of nonsense with a bunch of nothing yo-yo's than I ever spent with Mr. Big. I still don't think he realizes how well I could do his job, and now he'll never know because he never gave me a chance to tell him. Like I say, they're an idiot company."

Smith is completely unaware that he badly failed the test with the chauffeur, receptionist, Mr. Medium, and all the others he met. He doesn't realize that Mr. Big's time is too valuable to be wasted on losers or lost causes. Once he got everybody's failing mark on Smith, Mr. Big gave him a minimum polite audience and washed him out. There was nothing that Smith could have said to salvage the situation, as Mr. Big wasn't about to waste further time by listening to Smith's harangue about his competence.

The most unfortunate part of all this is that Smith learned absolutely nothing from his experience. Compatibility and objectivity are still not part of his lexicon. He still doesn't know what an interview is all about, and he will go on making the same error indefinitely. His habit pattern of mistakes and ignorance will be repeated in future interviews and become so ingrained that Smith will have made himself virtually unemployable.

Interview
Do's and Don'ts

TALKING

Most interviewees not only talk about the wrong things, such as competence, they talk too much. They get nervous if there are a few seconds of silence and feel the need to jump in with some kind of sales pitch or offer gratuitous commentary of some kind. This propensity may fill the gap of silence, but it accomplishes little beyond that. The interviewee needs facts. The interviewer already knows a good deal about him or her through the up-front checkings that resulted in just a handful out of hundreds of applicants being brought in for audience. The interviewee may have been objectively thorough about his homework, looking up the company in various directories. But the data he came by are merely statistics —Standard Industrial Classification numbers, sales volume, capitalization, numbers of employees, plant and branch locations, etc. These figures do not indicate how the business is run or what the policy and climate may be.

The interviewer is establishing the compatibility of the applicant to that climate. Because compatibility is a two-way street, it behooves the candidate to find out if the work environment and climate are going to be compatible for him, too. Can he be happy with the policy, the way the business is run? Maybe the ethics aren't of the highest order. The candidate might view them as sleazy and uncomfortable to work with.

As mentioned earlier, it does not matter how well a person can do a job or how well he is paid to do it. If that person isn't happy in his work, it is not a career, or even a job. It's a jail sentence. The candidate must pick up enough information about how the business is run to enable him to make a rational decision as to whether or not he should take the job if it is offered. He cannot do this by talking. To learn what he needs to know, he must listen.

If the applicant is talking 50 percent of the time, and most candidates talk much more, he will not have gotten enough data about the policy and climate of the company to make an intelligent decision as to whether he can happily and comfortably spend the rest of his years in its employ. Even a 60–40 split is only a fair interview. A good interview is one in which the applicant talks 25 percent of the time to the interviewer's 75 percent. If the candidate can control the interview so that he is only talking 10 percent of the time to the interviewer's 90 percent, it is a great interview. He has practically guaranteed his getting the offer and knows whether or not he should accept. We'll show you how to achieve this a little later.

Remember not to oversell, to talk yourself past the point of closure and out of the sale. However polished a sales pitch may be, overdoing it, coming on with too much of a good thing, can raise objections in the mind of the listener. The role of any salesman is to overcome buyer objection, not to introduce new objections because of overtalking. "Don't buy yet, I haven't finished my spiel."

An interview is very definitely a sales mission, so don't talk too much. Sit out silences of even thirty seconds or more without becoming a verbal activist. Let the interviewer break the silence. The interlude of quiet could be quite deliberate on the interviewer's part to evaluate your restraint, control, and poise. If you jump in nervously after a few seconds of silence and start rattling like an empty wagon, you may very well be failing a test of your patience.

A final word on the dangers of talking too much in an interview: Remember that nature equipped us with two ears and only one tongue. Without meaning to sound profound, we think there could be some significance to that. At the very least, as you go into interviews you'll be carrying with you some handy reminders to listen more and talk less.

ATTITUDE

Most applicants at an interview project a negative and self-disqualifying image. They figuratively sit at a distance from the interviewer, with the desk between them acting as a barrier or a chasm. They talk in terms of I and you (the interviewer and his company) in "never the twain shall meet" fashion. They relate too much to the past, not recognizing that the interviewer is interested in, and buying, the future. They concentrate on describing their experience and skills. They tell how they might be of possible use should they somehow be given the job which they don't really expect to happen because they haven't had any luck at all in their many previous interviews. This negativism is communicable and will rub off on the interviewer, with unhappy results.

An interviewee should proceed positively, conveying the impression that he expects to be hired, giving the interviewer credit for enough intelligence to recognize a good thing when he sees it. The interviewee should bridge the gap between him and the interviewer by projecting ahead positively as he talks. "Once I'm aboard we can . . . ," "For the next fall season we'll want to prepare . . . ," or "For the remainder of this year we'll have to continue the current marketing plan, but for next year we'll want to . . . ."

The interviewee should not be afraid that this attitude will be perceived as unwelcome presumption. He should know that managers are expected to display an upbeat, optimistic attitude as they go about their business. After all, they do establish the climate for their subordinates and their share of the overall operation. Any manifestations of uncertainty and pessimism on the part of a manager are highly contagious, and will very quickly infect and affect everyone around him. As gloom and doom are never welcome anywhere, care should be taken to avoid projecting either during the interview.

APPROACH

No interviewer regards himself and his company as an extension of the welfare state or as a social agency whose mission is to solve your personal problems for you. He couldn't care less about your problems. His only interest is in what you can do for his company. Can you make money, save money, solve problems? Can you do it all compatibly, as a good team member? Never talk about your wants, needs, preferences, family problems, or the money you need to meet your overhead and pay for your kid's college tuition. You would be viewed by the interviewer as a loner, self-centered, subjective, and naive. Confine your conversation to the company, its interests, and its problems. Project yourself as a money-making, money-saving problem solver. Show that you realize that the company's mission is to make a profit, not to take care of you and your problems.

THE WORD "I"

The most reprehensible word in the English language is the first person pronoun "I." Because of excessive subjectivity, it is heavily overused, without the speaker realizing how tiresome it is. Worse yet, it conveys a self-centered, self-concerned attitude, which is hardly what the interviewer is looking for. He wants a good team member, so sound like one by avoiding the use of the word "I." Use editorial plurals instead — we, us, our, together we can. Use possessive pronouns — my background, our mission, my group was responsible for. Your accomplishments were probably not achieved alone anyway, so why create false impressions or appear to be trying to hog all the glory? For every star ball carrier there are ten other very necessary guys doing the blocking. If you are not a Larry Csonka or a Franco Harris, don't try to pretend you are. There are a lot of other less visible and less publicized positions to be filled on All-Pro teams besides running back. Try to act and sound like a team player by staying away from the first person pronoun. Use plurals and possessives instead.

CHOICE OF WORDS

Remember that the interviewer is trying to come by some perception of the kind of person the candidate is and how he will conduct himself on the job. If the applicant uses strong, harsh words, the interviewer is going to equate this as meaning he can expect strong, harsh action from him. He may not want this; in fact, such words may frighten him. Maybe he hopes to hire someone who will make waves and rock the boat, but he doesn't want the boat to be swamped or capsized. If a candidate uses words like "cease," "desist," "raze," "sharpen," "tighten," "restructure," "discontinue," or "cancel," the interviewer may visualize a bull in a china shop or a new broom stirring up clouds of dust, with all the help in a tizzy and a lot of downtime.

The interviewer would prefer things to be done smoothly, with some fancy footwork instead of a bulldozer approach. He wants a minimum of fuss, so use mild, moderate words that won't frighten him — words like "polish," "hone," "refine," "modify," "phase out," and "revise." Persuade him that you are a smoothie, not a Sherman tank, and that you'll do your work quietly and in a low-keyed fashion.

PRESSURE

Two of the hardest things for any manager to do are to hire and fire people. Even though you're out and he's in, the interview is going to be difficult for the interviewer too, not just for you, the interviewee. Keep that in mind, and do your best to decompress the interview, to relieve the pressure, to keep things low-keyed.

Remember that the man before you cannot make the hiring decision alone. Recognize that you will be seeing a group of people, none of whom can make a unilateral decision. You want to keep getting invited back for further interviews, however many, until the process stops. There is no way of predetermining how long this will take or how many people will be involved. You may be interviewed by two or three officers at the division level, then by two or three more at the corporate level. The lower-level people you may have met earlier — chauffeur, receptionist, Mr. Medium, etc. — merely assisted in determining whether the decision-making group interview process should be started.

Don't ever crowd or push any single member of this decision-making group into making a hiring decision; the only decision he or she can make alone is a negative one. The chain, the continuity, can be broken if you are not passed on to the next person. You would no longer be under consideration. Not only shouldn't you ask the question directly, or even indirectly — don't even use body language or a facial expression to ask if you have the job. Play the game, run out the string, by making it easy for each person to relay you along.

At some point you will have seen the necessary number of participants. They will put their heads together, compare notes, and agree: "We all think he's great, so what are we waiting for? Let's hire him." Your only chance for this happy event is to decompress your interviews/audiences with the group members. Pressure any of them and you won't be passed along; you'll be shown the door instead.

Phases of the Interview

Keep in mind that the interview is not all loose, conversational exchange. Instead it is quite structured, and consists of three phases. In the first phase the interviewee must find out the problems and what the prospective employer hopes to have done about them. It will almost always be conducted by the man to whom you will be reporting, the man for whom you will be working. During this phase you learn the policy and climate under which the operation is conducted, so that you can decide if you want to work there if you do get the job offer. Your exploration now will also cue and slant your answers during Phase Two.

Phase Two will begin with the same man. He has asked you to submit a pro forma prospectus on the problems you learned about during Phase One. Next, you'll be talking about yourself, answering a lot of questions that are a common denominator in almost all interviews. If you pass, the person interviewing you, Mr. Big, will invite you back to talk to his boss, Mr. Big-Big, or whomever is next on the list.

Phase Three takes place after you have successfully gotten by all the people in the group that has the collective responsibility for hiring. They have agreed that you are the man for the job. Now you go back to Mr. Big to negotiate, to play the numbers game. This is only logical, since you'll be working for him, and will be part of his budget. He deserves the chance to try to get you for as little money as possible. Whatever he works out with you he'll have to live with. His associates, who participated in deciding favorably on you, are going to keep their hands off the way he spends his budget money.

PHASE ONE: EARLY PITFALLS

The chauffeur, the receptionist, Mr. Medium, and the others you have talked to have given you a passing grade, and you now have an appointment with Mr. Big. He has received favorable reports on you; you are not a lost cause. You are not about to get Smith's short shrift, the five-minutes-and-out treatment. But you've got a long way to go before coming up a winner, and much to do en route.

After a moment or two of warm-up conversation, during which Mr. Big is sizing up your overt characteristics, the interview proper will begin with Mr. Big saying, "Well, tell me about yourself, Mr. Hopeful." This is the first trap. Many unknowing applicants regard it as an invitation to recount their life histories. They start by saying they were born in Big Town, grew up on sidewalks, worked as a paper boy or in a drugstore after school, and spent their summers at their uncle's chicken farm. It never occurs to them that Mr. Big may only have budgeted a couple of hours for the interview. What a crime it is to waste this precious time on irrelevancies!

When Mr. Big asks about you, he is usually trying to evaluate how knowledgeable you are about the structure of the interview. If a candidate permits Phase One to be skipped, he is doing himself a disservice. When he talks later, he'll be mostly off target, playing guessing games, stabbing around without knowing what he should be talking about, wasting Mr. Big's valuable time even more.

Even if Mr. Big is proceeding subjectively, trying to satisfy his needs and wants with a minimum expenditure of time, effort, and energy, and is trying to cut the interview short, there is another reason the candidate should not help him. Remember, he has to catch up to Mr. Big, who already knows a great deal about him. The candidate needs to find out how the business is run so he can decide whether the climate and environment are compatible to him. He'll never find out by talking. He's got to get Mr. Big talking, and listen.

So, in response to Mr. Big's "Tell me about yourself" request, you should reply, "There is so much to tell you about myself I hardly know where to begin. I certainly don't want to waste your valuable time talking about immaterial things. If you'll describe your problem, Mr. Big, and what you hope somebody can do about it, I'll excerpt out of my background and experience those things that are relevant, saving a great deal of your time."

If Mr. Big is a knowledgeable, objective interviewer you will have passed with this answer, which demonstrates your own objectivity and awareness of what the interview is all about. Even if Mr. Big is proceeding subjectively he cannot quarrel with your logic and reasoning. He will also respond favorably to your concern for his time. And the more subjective he is, the more he'll be interested in talking about himself, his job, his problems, his company—they're his favorite topics. Either way, you will have avoided the trap and passed the evaluation. You will have hit Mr. Big on the "on" button and gotten him talking instead of you so that you can learn what you need to know to make compatibility judgments later.

Keep Mr. Big talking as long as possible. The more he talks, the more you'll learn. You'll be hearing things that will reveal the size of the puddle you'll be in, that will clue you on ball-park salary brackets if this is a "salary negotiable" situation. You'll be getting firm information as to what the company will expect from you. You'll be getting some perceptions about the policy and climate of the business and how it is conducted.

If Mr. Big runs down, rewind him. One of the best ways to do this is to ask pertinent questions. There is no better way to demonstrate that you are with his subject and him than to pose one-liner queries. "Did you ever think of putting the framis ahead of the razzmatazz?" Mr. Big replies, "We've had the framis right up tight behind the razzmatazz but never ahead of it," and he's off and running again.

Don't ever interrupt Mr. Big with long dissertations of your own. These would be premature and indicate high subjectivity on your part. You'll get your chance to talk in Phase Two, so give Mr. Big his turn without disturbing or distracting him. Above all, don't introduce any topic that does not relate to the problem Mr. Big is describing. Keep him concentrating on himself, his job, his company, his problems.

Mr. Big might tell you, "We've got a product line that is beautifully designed and engineered. Our production is of the highest quality. But we're getting killed by a lot of misuse out in the field because our explanatory literature is not clear enough. We need someone to completely revise our support print. We need crystal-clear graphics and schematics instead of what we have now, which isn't doing the job.

"We want this same man to run seminars for the salesmen of our various distributors around the country. We must make sure they understand the products' use, and can impart the facts to their customers. As part of the seminar we want our man to do market research by asking the guys out on the firing line — these distributor salesmen — what they would like to have from us as additions to the line. We figure it will take our man about two years to get all this done. At the end of that time we plan to transfer him to our research and development section in Weeweehootchie, Mississippi, as our new products manager with a raise to $25,000."

What a gold mine of information you've picked up—their timetable, ball-park salary figures, a forewarning of heavy travel, and future plans! A negative aspect has also appeared. You may not want to move to Weeweehootchie. On the other hand, it would be counterproductive and pointless for you to mention it at this early juncture. When they have decided you are the man for the job and you're back with Mr. Big to play the numbers game in Phase Three, that is the time to negotiate the Weeweehootchie matter, not before.

The matter must be disposed of, however. Do not take the job in the hope that when the time comes you'll somehow be able to wriggle out of going. That would be unethical. Weeweehootchie is one of the conditions of the job. If you can't eliminate Weeweehootchie through negotiation, and you can't go there, for whatever reason, don't take the job. But do wait for Phase Three before you bring up the problem. If they want you badly, it'll be easier for you to get out of going.

As Mr. Big warms up to his topic during Phase One he is very likely to give you a tour of the premises and particularly to show you the problem spot. En route to the trouble scene, do not distract Mr. Big by gratuitously offering commentary about the splendid housekeeping, the sunlit premises, or the great sanitation. Aside from the fact that Mr. Big may interpret these remarks as an attempt at ingratiation, which he may not care for, you'd be distracting him from his worries and problems, which are what you want him to concentrate on. Don't sweat if there are considerable intervals of silence along the way. Let Mr. Big break the silence. Don't jump in nervously, interrupting his show and derailing his train of thought. It won't help your cause, and if the tour silences are deliberate, it will downgrade an estimation of your self-restraint and patience.

At the trouble spot you'll be given a rundown on the problem by Mr. Big and by some of the people who are responsible and who are trying to cope. After they have finished, you may well be asked what you think needs to be done to rectify matters. If you take a stab at the solution and arrive at the right one, you've eliminated your prospective job. They don't need you anymore, as you've given them a free consultation.

You will also be seen as a bit of a wise guy. Here these people have been wrestling with the problem for heaven only knows how long, and you come up with a solution after the briefest of exposures to it, without even getting into all the factors that make up the problem. This is demeaning to Mr. Big and his subordinates, and hardly a way to score Brownie points.

Lastly, and most important of all, you will be perceived as lacking objectivity. Subjective managers are the ones who shoot from the hip. They are the ones who don't diagnose their problems thoroughly before prescribing solutions. Part of Mr. Big's problem is that he already has too many subjective managers around the premises and he certainly doesn't want or need any more.

If they insist and there's no way you can avoid giving them your early perceptions, be sure to qualify and requalify everything you say so that you cannot be accused of being subjective. "Objective managers don't go off half-cocked or play guessing games when they don't know all the factors involved. From what's been seen and heard so far, it would seem that if we put the framis up ahead of the razzmatazz it should improve matters. But once I'm aboard and we have had a chance to research the problem completely, we'll undoubtedly want to revise this very early guesstimate." This kind of response would be highly appropriate.

Mr. Big will introduce you to the people operating in the problem area. In fact, he might very well leave you with them and go back to his office. These people are part of the team evaluating your objectivity and compatibility. They'll each ask a few questions chosen from public areas of interest and concern. In many cases these questions will be assigned so as to avoid duplication.

Mr. Big may leave you with a Mr. White, who will give you a rundown on his portion of the operation. Sandwiched into the discussion will be the evaluative questions. You will probably be asked what you think of Mr. Big. You might be tremendously impressed by him and be tempted to reply, "He's the greatest genius since Michelangelo and I can hardly wait to sit at his knee and sop up knowledge from him." Aside from being obsequious overkill, such a comment would reveal subjective prejudgment. You'd be reaching your conclusion too soon to be considered objective. You don't know Mr. Big

114

well enough yet to make that kind of judgment. A better answer would be, "Speaking from my short exposure to him, Mr. Big would seem to be a very knowledgeable man. It is my hope that once I'm aboard and under his direction some meaningful contributions to the team effort will come quickly."

Mr. White may now pass you along to a Mr. Brown, who will also talk about the operation. He may also slip in a couple of people questions, such as "What do you think of Mr. White?" You might be totally unimpressed by Mr. White and feel he is incompetent. But you can't say so. You could be right. White may be on his way out, kept only until you've been aboard long enough to get your feet wet. But you can't belabor the point. You don't know if this is going to happen, and you don't want to make snap judgments. You might be wrong. Maybe White doesn't make a good first impression, but you may learn in time to respect and admire him, just as everyone else around the place does.

Stay safely on middle ground by replying, "We only spent a very short time together, but Mr. White seems to be the kind of man an objective manager like myself can relate to and get along with. (As an objective manager you should be able to get along with anyone, so that is an accurate statement.) Once I'm aboard it is my hope that we will be able to fit our shoulders together into the same team harness and between us pull a pretty good load." You might pull 75 percent of the load to his 25 percent. White might surprise you by pulling his half. You might also be shocked to find that White is pulling 75 percent of the load by himself. These are matters that can only be discovered later. Any guesses you might make at this point in time would be premature and unhelpful.

At any rate, Mr. Brown may leave you with Mr. Green, who later takes you to Mr. Blue, and so on. Stay in the objective middle with all these people as you respond to their questions. Ultimately this referral game will end, and you'll find yourself back in Mr. Big's office. He will have been getting favorable reports on you from the people you have met. You'll be rated objective, compatible, interpersonally skilled, and a probable excellent manager of people. You are almost at the end of Phase One.

Mr. Big will say, "Well, Mr. Hopeful, you've spent a lot of time with us learning about our operation and our problems. What I'd like you to do is give what you've seen and heard some thought, and then write up a pro forma prospectus on what you think should be done. Do you think you could get this finished in time to meet with me again next Tuesday at 10 A.M.?" Your answer is obviously affirmative. And you should be pleased. You've passed all the tests so far, and accomplished your mission of getting invited back.

Go home and write up what you think should be done. Don't worry about the content of what you write. It is your approach that will count. How you handle the prospectus will be another test of your flexibility. Take the known facts of the problem and use them as a base. If the unknowns you uncover with further investigation after you've been hired point in such and such a direction, option A is suggested. If the unknowns turn out to be headed another way, option B may be the solution. If they go in a third direction, option C may be the way to go.

Three alternatives are enough. They will prove your flexibility, your objectivity. Don't worry about the accuracy of your forecasts. These are not being monitored, nor will you be criticized later if you are somewhat off target with your projections. You might be surprised and a bit unhappy when you bring back your prospectus and Mr. Big only gives it a glance. Once he has seen that you've come up with options and alternatives, he will be satisfied.

To repeat: Mr. Big doesn't care about the content or accuracy of your forecast. He is only interested in *how* you answered. If you had come up with just one answer, you'd have flunked, even if it turned out to be exactly right and dead on target. He might figure it as just a lucky stab, not likely to be repeated. Remember, what he is looking for is objectivity. He'd rather see plural options, with none of them right, than a single accurate guesstimate.

The distance factor bears heavily on the way the interview will be conducted. If you live nearby, and only a short trip by car or public transportation is involved, the interview will usually be broken up into a number of separate visits. You will meet different people at different times. However, after you are interviewed by the officers of the local division, further interviews might be scheduled with a couple of corporate officers in some distant city. If the level of your position warrants such interviews you can expect to see the pertinent officers on the same single trip to headquarters, either together or spaced out over a day or so. They will coordinate their time and schedules rather than have you fly back and forth a couple of times. Aside from the waste of plane fare, such shuttling would be highly unbusinesslike and unprofessional, and would reveal poor planning.

If you are interviewing for a job in a distant city, one that involves relocation, things will be different. Be prepared for a possible marathon. They may bring you in early in the morning, run through lunch, all afternoon, dinner, then on into the evening, with a possible tour of night spots finishing off a very long day. During this time, you will meet everyone who is involved in making the decision on you. They'll be taking turns at you, in relays, maybe in groups. They may leave the proceedings for a while and rejoin them later. They can be a lot fresher and less drained than you, as they will have some respite, some relief. You, unfortunately, are going to be on stage the whole time. There will be no breaks, no recesses, not even at mealtimes. Just because you've left the business premises to go to lunch still doesn't mean you can relax. You have to be more alert and on guard than ever.

For example, by prior arrangement you as the stranger in the group will be approached by the waiter or waitress with the inevitable "Something from the bar, gentlemen?" If you order a drink, you hosts/companions will refrain to see how you handle being tipped off balance. If you don't order a drink, they will, for the same reason. You can help yourself by saying, "Gentlemen, I usually don't drink at lunch. But there are some occasions when for public relations or other purposes a drink is indicated. Is this such an occasion?" Let them make the decision.

If they abstain, you abstain, even though you might dearly like a drink because of the strain you've been under. If they order, you order, but get the longest, tallest drink you can think of. A Bloody Mary, a tall scotch and water, or a tall bourbon and soda would be suitable. If you're thirsty dig into your water glass, not your drink. Whatever you've ordered has to last throughout the entire meal, as you're only going to have that one libation. Sip slowly. If you get too far down into the glass you're apt to be enticed into playing chugalug and having a refill, and then maybe a third.

You think you're with a bunch of lushes, but you're anxious to please, so you go along. Meanwhile, you're showing a lack of objective moderation. Your hosts may not go the three-cocktail route again until the next time they interview somebody of your caliber. They've been seducing you, and you've been proving you can be blandished away from objective moderation. When you have two or three drinks at a business lunch you're no longer working, you're playing.

All you had to do to identify was to have one drink. You'd then have joined up and been one of the boys. You could not be thought of as sitting there abstemiously looking down your long, blue, superior nose at lesser beings who have not conquered the vice of alcohol as you have. On the other hand, if you have more than one drink, even if you're only following their example, you're striking out.

Sure, they have some concern for the size of your expense account. But they are more concerned about your behavior, your health, and the possibility of a lot of on-the-job absenteeism on your part. They see lost afternoons if you entertain at lunch a lot and go the three double Beefeater martini route every day. They might also worry about some fuzzy-minded, fuzzy-tongued inadvertent revelations of confidential information on your part. So be one of the boys, but not a playboy. Have only one drink at lunch.

Your marathon distant-city interview might see you going out to dinner with the same, or, more likely, another, group. The fact that you're now even tireder and could use a pick-me-up, the fact that it is now dark and after business hours, the fact that you don't usually drink at lunch but at night when you're home or traveling alone you usually have a couple plus a splash dividend — none of these changes the reality, which is that you're still on stage, still being interviewed, still being evaluated. So you only have one drink, the way you did at lunchtime. You've apparently gotten pretty far down the track successfully, so don't blow the whole bit at this late stage of the game.

If you're not going to have to do much entertaining on the job you may be spared the tour of the town. But if you will be in sales, marketing, or any other meet-the-public capacity, you may very well find yourself and your hosts doing the night spots, catching a combo here, a vocalist there, a floor show somewhere else. Naturally, every place you go, you've got to order a drink. But you don't have to drink it. Don't worry about your host's money, or the old "willful waste makes woeful want" bit. Stick your tongue in your drinks, spit in them, spoil them, do anything except drink them.

You may have had to get up at 5 in the morning to catch the flight that brought you here at 9 A.M. to begin your marathon. Nervousness and apprehension may have prevented you from sleeping well to begin with. Your chemistry has been working overtime for a lot of long, pressure-packed hours. Maybe under ordinary circumstances you can handle a half-dozen drinks without turning a hair. But now the drinks and the agitated state of your endocrinology combine to convince you that your companions have fallen in love with you at first sight, largely because of your charming personality.

You decide to be even more charming, and you overdo it, you depart from the area of objective moderation. You tell your favorite off-color jokes or you sing the dirty ditties you learned in the service. You become a stand-up comic. Whatever the manifestation, you're striking out, and very late in the game. It's the bottom of the ninth, and you're losing after being ahead for eight innings.

On your night-spot tours, be moderate in the hours you keep, also. When it gets to be about 11 o'clock figure out how you can cut out. Say your group is about to leave one place for another at 11:15 P.M. Tell your hosts, "This has been great fun and I've enjoyed myself a lot. But it is getting late and we've got to meet again tomorrow morning, so I'm going to grab a cab back to the hotel. Besides, I promised my wife I'd give her a call before midnight. Go on if you'd like, but I'm going to leave the party. It's been a long day." You'll find that your hosts will happily call a halt to the proceedings and go home, too. And you have passed another test. You proved that as a front man for this company, you can do all the entertaining required of you and finish it before midnight.

You must exercise control over excesses. If you do not, and succumb to the importunings of a client you're entertaining, you may find yourself and that client in some joint at about 2:30 in the morning. You're handling your liquor well, but your client is getting smashed. He's the one who is coming on like a stand-up comic. Worse yet, he makes a pass at some woman in the place, and her boyfriend lands a right on his jaw. All of a sudden, you've got someone on your hands with a busted jaw that is going to have to be wired, along with other troubles. You're into a real bad scene, which could have been avoided by making like Cinderella and getting both you and your client home before midnight.

True, a fracas can get started before midnight, but the odds aren't as great as they are after midnight. Go with the percentages and go home early. Control situations, time, and clients through the exercise of objective moderation. You'll not only be holding down expenses, you'll be holding down the potential for mishap. You and your career will have a better chance to survive, and therefore to prosper. Don't "me too" along. Ignore blandishments by prospective employers, clients, or anyone else that will lead you to extremes. You could gain nothing and lose everything. Keep away from the outer limits of things. You might just slip and fall off. Stick to the safe, solid, middle ground.

PHASE TWO:
YOU AND YOUR PROSPECTIVE EMPLOYER

It is now Tuesday and you are back with Mr. Big, prospectus in hand. You are disappointed because he paid so little attention to it once he saw that you came up with three alternative solutions to the problem. You worked long and hard on your answers and gave them a lot of thought. You thought he was going to evaluate seriously the options you presented. You did not recognize that the prospectus was merely a check of your flexibility, to show that you would not make a premature effort to arrive at a viable game plan.

This preliminary over with, Mr. Big will give you your turn to talk by asking a lot of personal questions. These questions are a common denominator in all the Phase Two interviews you will have with all the people involved in the hiring decision. We will list these questions in logical order. But don't be disturbed if question two appears seventh or vice versa. The sequence may be quite random and scrambled, but however acrobatical the order, they'll all get asked.

You want to prepare and polish your replies. After perfecting them commit them to memory, so that you tell the same story to everyone you meet in Phase Two. If you answer one interviewer one way, a later interviewer another way, and a still later interviewer a third way, you're dead. These people will get together to compare notes. If everybody has heard a different story, there'll be total confusion in the group. The only thing they will be able to agree on is not to hire you. If you are consistent in your answers, they will have a basis for comparison. Your consistency will meet with their approval, and help them to agree. The decision will be, "What are we waiting for? Let's hire him."

The first question is apt to be "What prompted you to approach us (or answer our ad), of all the companies in the industry (or the world)?" In replying to this you cannot talk about the benefits you hope to receive. You can't say you've suddenly realized you have nothing laid by for your retirement or old age. You know this company has the greatest package of fringe benefits anywhere, so you want to join up and latch onto some of these goodies to make up for your earlier neglect. Neither can you say that the company has the greatest product since sliced bread, that selling it will be like shooting fish in a barrel, and that you figure you can make twice as much money as you've ever made before with only half the effort.

You may be voicing your honest opinion, but it won't

get you hired. Neither can you confess that you've been out of work for a long time and you're broke. You've decided to grab the first halfway decent offer that comes along so you can get off the street and get some of your bills paid. Mr. Big will assume you regard the situation he's offering as a stopgap measure, and that once you've caught up on your debts and have built up a reserve you'll be out looking for something better.

What Mr. Big hopes to hear is that by some selection process unknown to him you have picked out his company and only a handful of others to approach, with a long-term career involvement in mind. He has no interest in your personal problems. He does not regard his company as an extension of the welfare state whose only reason for being is your benefit. His only interest in you is in what you can do for him. Can you make money for him? Can you save money for him? Can you solve his problems for him? Can you do it all compatibly? You've got to answer in terms of what he is looking for and hopes to hear from you. You've got to talk his language, not yours.

Accordingly, your response to his "why us" question should be, "Everybody knows your company and the fine reputation you have in the industry, and how you're growing to the point where you'll be number one in just a few more years. That is why I approached you. I'm a go-and-grow person, so we'd be very compatible. It just seemed to me to be a natural for us to join together and get to be number one in the industry together. Perhaps with me aboard we could do it a little faster."

A reply of this kind contains the right, magic words all your interviewers want to hear. Also, you answered in a positive, upbeat fashion, you mentioned and showed awareness of the key word "compatible," and you have projected a team-player image. And there was little use of the first person pronoun "I."

The next questions from Mr. Big will probably be, "Where do you see this company and this industry going five, ten, and fifteen years from now and what do you think we will have to do to retain what should be our lead position by that time?" Here again how you answer rather than content is the important consideration. Nobody is going to monitor, to measure the accuracy of your present forecasting at some future date, saying "You claimed we'd be at point X in five years and here we are at point Y instead. How come?"

Take literary license. Use your imagination. Show a step-by-step progression from five to ten to fifteen years, hanging it all together. Do not neglect the problems apt to be encountered en route. Mention them and state broadly what could be done about them without getting into details and techniques.

In other words, don't give a careless answer or come up with nothing but blue-sky recitation. Include the probable bad news as well. You'll have time to ponder futures of this kind before the interview, so do your homework and prepare an upbeat, imaginative, positive projection. What Mr. Big is checking is your attitude and anticipation. Do you think and plan ahead? Do you operate with the long-range global overview of a top-level executive? Or are you basically a technician, oriented toward the task and the expedient handling of current problems alone?

Mr. Big knows he can determine a man's caliber, what he has been, what he is capable of, by his approach to problems. The candidate's prior titles are not that informative if only because of semantic variations. A man who by nature limits his problem approaches to "how" — how do we do it better, faster, or cheaper — belongs in lower management or technical management. A man who addresses himself to "why" problems — why are we doing it this way, why wouldn't that way be better — is exhibiting the attitudes of middle management. The man who addresses himself to finding answers to the "what" questions — what share of the market do we want five years from now, what additions to the line are we going to need to accomplish this, what kind of added facility and personnel will we need, what kind of financing will be required — is of top-level management caliber even if he has not yet reached his potential.

If Mr. Big and his company are dynamic and running on a fast track, and if they promote from within as much as possible, as most companies prefer, Mr. Big is looking ahead and wondering about your upward mobility potential. If you give him the impression that you have limited promotability because you're a "how" person, he may not hire you. It would be a poor business investment on his part to bring in a man who has already reached his plateau. And you would not be happy with your static position and career, either. You would not realize that your own limited attitude, not a lack of opportunity, was at fault. Mr. Big doesn't have time to remake you, to educate you, to change your habitual posture and stance. For your sake as well as his, it would be easier for him not to hire you and to continue his search for a better, more upward mobile fit.

So, wherever you are in the business hierarchy and whatever your title, if you've been addressing yourself solely to "how" problems, stop. Start preparing yourself for promotion by paying attention to the higher-level questions of "why" and "what." The redirection of your thinking will be noticed because the company is looking for it, whether you've realized it before or not. It will be rewarded, too, as it should be, provided your superiors have not given you up as hopelessly and unchangeably typecast and "sot in concrete." If they don't notice that you've changed for the better, you would be well advised to pack up the new you, pack in, and move on.

Mr. Big's third question will be in the same vein: "Where do you see yourself fitting into this picture five, ten, fifteen years from now?" Even though it may be your goal, you cannot indicate to Mr. Big that in five years you're going to have his job, in ten years you're going to be executive vice president, and in fifteen years you want to be president. Never target on any specific job title. Mr. Big isn't going to hire any threat to himself or some of his crony associates.

Nor should you describe the benefits or compensation you hope to attain. Many men make the mistake of saying that in five years they'd like to be making $50,000, in ten years $100,000, and in fifteen years $200,000. They hope to enjoy salaries in those ranges, but they make it sound like largesse because they haven't said what they'll do to deserve such munificence. At any rate, these answers are not slanted toward Mr. Big and his company. They are highly subjective, and as a consequence are poorly regarded.

A proper reply would be, "Mr. Big, my objective is to help your company make money, save money, and solve problems. Where my career winds up, and with what title, isn't important, just so my progress takes me somewhere close to the top with some voice in making policy decisions. Compensation is no worry. If I succeed in making and saving money for the company, my earnings will be taken care of. In fact, Mr. Big, if you're hoping to become president someday, I'd sure like to help you get there."*

You have not posed a threat to Mr. Big or any of his buddies. On the contrary, you've related to him as your boss (the name of the game) and offered to help him reach the top. You haven't set your sights on any particular job title or position. You've indicated that you hope to

---

*By the way, as you are interviewed by other members of the decision-making group, don't tell them you'd like to help them become president. Reserve that offer for the boss immediately ahead of you, the man to whom you'll be reporting. Obviously, that kind of comment would not fit or apply to the other interviewers. You can't be all things to all people, so don't try. Circumstances and bosses may change, but at this point Mr. Big is your only pipeline into the system and into what will be going on above you. He's the only one you should offer to help.

achieve upward mobility and reward through your ability and efforts. You've conveyed flexibility as a team guy, prepared to do what circumstances require. Your goals are realistic and objective. Who can tell what you will be doing in fifteen years anyway? Besides, the closer you get to the top, the more of a generalist you will have to be. Lastly, there is little use of the word "I."

The next question will be an extension of the last two, but its purpose will be different. Mr. Big will ask, "What do you think of our competition, the ABC Company?" He might even bait you further by asking, "Are they as sleazy to compete against as they're said to be?" Whether the question is single- or double-barreled don't knock the other company. Don't bite on his bait and try to ingratiate yourself with: "When you're competing against them you're really rolling around in the mud, and you've got to use your sharpest pencil because they'll rebate, deal under the table, and use every dirty trick in the book." You've taken an extreme point of view. Worse, you've allowed yourself to be tricked into this inappropriate response. For all you know, Mr. Big's company is about to take over the ABC Company and you were being considered to act as merger liaison. Your commentary would disqualify you and would destroy your credibility for such a role.

Don't argue with Mr. Big either, denying that the ABC Company is sleazy. Instead, decompress the situation. Answer this loaded question with: "Well, Mr. Big, we all hear good and bad stories about every company in the industry, but I never pay much attention to backyard gossip. However they operate, there's plenty of room in the marketplace for them and for us. I just want to make sure we legitimately get a bigger share of that market than they do, that's all." Mr. Big will find nothing to quarrel about in this reply. You haven't bitten his lure, nor have you challenged his statement. Instead, you sidestepped his trap and stayed neutral. You've proved that you are adroit, that you are mentally fast on your feet, and that you know how to avoid potential trouble of an interpersonal nature.

Mr. Big might make a second effort by continuing, "Since you are familiar with the ABC Company, you must know my counterpart there, Henry Higgins. What do you know about him? Is he as much of a lush as they say he is?" Mr. Big might stop at "What do you know about him?" Or he may try to bait you into one-upsmanship by calling Henry Higgins a lush. Regardless, stay in the gray, objective middle — in other words don't reply that Higgins is not only a lush but a tomcat. Don't deny that Higgins is a lush. Whether he is or not may be purely a matter of opinion. To a complete teetotaler, a guy who has a dry sherry before lunch and dinner is a drinker. To someone who knocks off a fifth of scotch a day, a man who has two or three cocktails before lunch and dinner is merely observing the old health precept, "Don't eat on an empty stomach."

Mr. Big is not interested in picking up tidbits of gossip about his rival. He is interested in how you reply, not what you reply. Refrain from opening closet doors and rattling skeletons. Mr. Big probably knows a great deal more about Higgins than you do anyway. With all this in mind your reply should be, "Yes, I've gotten to know Higgins fairly well over the years. His company and my old one used to exhibit at the same conventions, and many years we found ourselves next-door, or across-the-aisle, neighbors. It is true that Higgins used to close an awful lot of hospitality suites at these conventions, but he was always down on the exhibit floor bright and early the next morning. Everything he does is always at full gallop. He works hard and he plays hard — that's his style."

Once more you have demonstrated nice restraint. Mr. Big was testing your trustworthiness, among other things, and you did not project like a gossipy washer-woman or a potential blackmailer. Mr. Big is understandably concerned about his reputation and what you might say about him if you later leave him or are separated for some reason. Mr. Big knows that once you get to know him well you might discover that he, too, has feet of clay, maybe all the way up to his knees. It is his hope you'll mercifully keep quiet about any failings or weaknesses he may later demonstrate. What you've just shown is that you are an aware, reliable, card-carrying member of the Professional Managers Mutual Benevolent and Protective Society.

All members of the PMMBPS recognize that they will occasionally witness some untoward, even irresponsible, behavior on the part of another card-carrying member. If they make a big thing of it, bruit it about, the offending member might lose his job, wind up with a broken marriage, or suffer other bad effects. So they protect him and keep quiet. Naturally, all bets are off if the offender becomes a frequent repeater, as the witnesses don't want to act as steady cover-ups for him. An occasional transgression is forgiven and forgotten; after all, we all have weak moments or bad days once in a while. In any case, Mr. Big knows that you understand and abide by this unwritten rule of restraint in your conduct.

Mr. Big's next question will probably be, "Why did you leave your last company?" He will then ask about why you left previous jobs. Here you've got to be careful. You don't want to project an image of an opportunistic buck chaser, ready to move any time anyone waves a few more dollars in the pay envelope at you. Refrain from using "more money" or "better opportunity" (which is the same thing) as your reason too many times. A change or two of this kind very early in your work history is okay, but don't make it sound as if your entire career has been made up of such job changes. Mr. Big is hoping for some stability, some reliability, from whomever he brings in. He does not want a job hopper.

Neither does he want anyone with a history of leaving jobs because of "personality clashes" or "philosophic differences," as these indicate high subjectivity. An objective person wouldn't have such problems. Mr. Big will also be turned off by a lot of solo separations, where you were the only person who left or was separated. He would suspect you of inflexibility, incompatibility, and an unwillingness on your part to adapt and adjust to your work environment. He would much prefer you to have been part of groups that left or were separated because of conditions beyond anyone's control, like the state of the economy.

Mr. Big will not take kindly to your calling former employers a bunch of crooks, or saying they used and abused you, never kept their promises to you, or were stupid or inept. He's automatically going to side with your former bosses, not you. He's a paid-in-full member of the Professional Managers Mutual Benevolent and Protective Society. Remember his concern about his image and reputation, and what you might say about him if you ever part company after he hires you.

Neither does Mr. Big want a suspicious, bitter person who is going to be so busy protecting himself that it will impair his effectiveness. So don't knock anybody — especially yourself. An interview is not a confessional box. You don't have to admit you were caught with your fingers in the till or misbehaving with your secretary.

Try to keep the reasons for your various job changes low key. Make it sound as if nobody was at fault, and certainly not you. It was "just one of those things." You can blame generic things, but not individuals or companies. "The military discontinued the weapons system our division was making, so the whole operation was shut down." "We were merged, with my company the mergee. The mergor already had my kind of guy aboard and there wasn't room for two of us, so obviously I went." "We got a new president. He understandably wanted to bring in his own team, so all of us in top management were replaced." "We lost our prime contract with one of the big syndicated variety-store chains and had to reduce staff by half. I didn't have enough seniority to be retained." "We were having some problems with nepotism and cronyism. Since nothing could be done about this situation, a lot of us gradually phased ourselves out over a period of a couple of years."

What you need to convey to Mr. Big is that your moves were made deliberately, and that you did not quit in a fit of anger, punching your boss in the nose for goodbyes. And, as mentioned earlier, try to keep your moves from sounding like the result of a confrontation. If other people around you left or were let go the same year you departed, you can water down the onus by saying "A group of us left," or "A half-dozen of us were gradually phased out over a year's time."

A final word of caution: Be brief about your reasons for change. If you run on to excessive length Mr. Big is going to think you're hiding something. You could wear out your welcome, too. He doesn't want your work life history, so state the facts quickly and broadly. Refer back to the various examples given. They don't belabor the point, they're short, and they're adequate. Anything more would be superfluous and counterproductive.

Mr. Big might then say, "Without naming the company it was for, which job did you like the most, and why?" In replying, don't talk about being your boss's pet, getting away with minimal performance, having memberships in luncheon clubs or country clubs, having company Cadillacs, or anything else in which the benefits are of such a personal nature. If you do, you'll be displaying the wrong attitude; you'll be deemed nothing but a spoiled free loader.

Instead, your response should be "Of all the places I've worked, there was one company that was really great. Communications were excellent. Everybody understood the goals and how it was proposed to meet them, so all managers were involved and knew what was expected of them. The whole operation was well planned and well implemented. Best of all, my boss was one of the most objective men I've ever worked for."

Don't be afraid to verbalize such words as objectivity, subjectivity, compatibility, and communications. Previously this terminology may not have been part of your usual lexicon. You now know that such words relate to what the interview is really all about, so talk Mr. Big's language. Let him see you understand the game you're both playing, and that you are not talking apples to his oranges.

The concomitant question to the last will be, "Of all the jobs you've had, which one did you like least and why?" You can't complain about low pay, too much work, too much travel, or anything else so personal. Keep in mind that Mr. Big is probing for and hoping to find objectivity. Accordingly, say, "The job I liked least was with a company that did little anticipating and forward planning. Consequently, goals were vague and kept changing almost from day to day with nobody knowing what was expected of them. Operating policy was completely one of expedience. Worst of all, my boss was one of the most subjective men I've ever met in business." You've let Mr. Big know the kind of work environments that turn you on and turn you off. You've also informed him that you are of a rare breed—you are an objective manager, just what he is looking for.

"What do you consider to be your greatest weakness?" might follow. This is no time to confess that you can't delegate authority and so have to do everything yourself, or that you find it difficult to accept orders, that you'd rather wing things your way. Even if it is true, don't say it. Your candor about the past is not being evaluated. And, hopefully, after reading this book you will have modified such previously weak areas for the better. Your improved understanding of the realities enables you to get rid of earlier hang-ups.

You can't deny having any weaknesses. That would be a sign of sheer fantasy and delusion, light-years away from reality. Nor can you express surprise and come up empty and without an answer, saying you never thought about the matter before. Such smug self-satisfaction would betray extreme subjectivity. Even a person of average subjectivity would not operate in a total vacuum. He would have some perceptions, some insights, some awareness of at least a few dents in his otherwise nicely rounded sphere. What you need to do is to acknowledge weakness but to convert it into an asset. Tell Mr. Big, "My weakness is that every time I have to fire one of my subordinates, it gets to me. I do it promptly so as not to waste the firm's money. But each time and without fail, I go off my feed and don't sleep well for a couple of weeks."

This is an acceptable weakness. Mr. Big wants you to be concerned about interpersonal matters. He does not want you sadistically prowling the premises, hatchet at hand, ready to hack off heads at the slightest provocation. Neither does he want you to procrastinate in such matters, hiding some guy who needs firing by sweeping him under the rug because you feel sorry for him or are worried about what his peers may think of you. If you acted that way you'd be abdicating your responsibility. You'd be leaking away the firm's money. Your reply should convince him that you'll do what has to be done without delay, but that you are not unfeeling and callous.

Pretty obviously, the corollary to the last question is, "What do you consider to be your greatest strength?" I'm sure you would have no trouble finding lots of attributes to mention. You could probably quite truthfully run down the Boy Scout oath: You're trustworthy, loyal, helpful, etc. But a recitation of worthy personality traits would be inappropriate and off-target. Instead, here is your chance to nail down the job.

Tell Mr. Big, "My greatest strength is my objectivity and consequent compatibility. I approach problems with an open, neutral mind, I'm thorough, I anticipate, and I'm flexible. I never shoot from the hip or make decisions off the top of my head. I manage by objective, objectively arrived at through options and alternatives." You have said it all. You have verbalized for Mr. Big, possibly better than he could have, all the things he's been groping for in the interview. Mr. Big can now break off the evaluation. You have passed with flying colors.

The interview may wind down with a few more information-gathering questions. To "What do you do to keep fit?" almost any reply will do, as long as you do something. You hike, bike, hunt, fish, swim, ski, bowl, play tennis, handball, golf, do calisthenics, isometrics, or lift weights. He merely wants reassurance that you're doing something to help your health, weight, circulation, and muscle tone. He does not want to hear that you spend all your spare time sprawled before the boob tube, a sedentary blob belting down beer by the six pack. He might worry that you have only a relatively short career before you until some cardiac or circulatory incoordination incapacitates you. Assure Mr. Big that you do something about physical fitness.

His next question will be about your hobbies or other interests. He hopes that you are not a hermit, confining yourself to your home or to one section of it. He'd rather not hear that you spend all your spare time in your den with high-intensity lamp, magnifying glass, and tweezers, poring over your stamp collection. He'd be happier to know that you are interested in civic or community activities of some sort, even if they are only with homely little neighborhood groups like the PTA, Little League, or Boy Scouts. Mentioning involvement with this kind of organization will allay any fear he might have that you may shun the many kinds of job-related social activities that are mandatory for management incumbents.

Perhaps in a very large city the managers of a company can get away with a minimum of rubber chicken, mashed potatoes, and peas nights, while listening to a lot of tedious talks about real or unrealistic civic concerns. In smaller cities that have only a handful of companies, with yours at or near the top of the list, you can bet that some member of your company's management team is going to be representing it in anything that goes on around town. You might wind up as a member of the ballet board or the symphony committee, or as a hospital trustee. These duties have to be divided up among the team, and Mr. Big would not relish hiring anyone unwilling to assume his proportionate share of the load.

Show him this is a bridge you've already crossed by describing what you've done of a community nature. If you haven't had involvements in work of this kind, mention how much you've always been interested in such matters and how much you're looking forward to making a meaningful contribution now.

Mr. Big will conclude Phase Two by taking you to lunch or dinner to meet his boss, Mr. Big-Big. Maybe you'll only meet Mr. Big-Big after lunch, or on another day. There's no way to tell in advance when the meeting will take place. To some extent it depends on such factors as how much of a hurry they are in to fill the slot and whether you live nearby or have come a long way. You might go straight to Mr. Big-Big and perhaps still another person before your interview day is done. You might be asked to come back tomorrow or next week if you live close by. Whatever the waiting time, you have accomplished your mission. You have been invited back to see the next person in the decision-making group. Your cause is alive.

As you are referred on, continue to keep a low-key profile and project an objective, positive attitude toward everyone and everything. Be sure to give them all the same answers to the same questions. Prepare and polish your responses in advance and commit them to memory, so that you present yourself in the best possible way to everyone concerned. We want truth in your package, but the package doesn't have to be a plain brown paper bag. Put on some fancy wrapping and ribbons. Give yourself some eye appeal and consistency to enable you to make it through Phase Two better. Once you've done that, Phase Three is relatively easy.

PHASE THREE: SALARY

Everyone else chosen to interview you has agreed that you should be hired. The end of referrals has been reached. The group concurs that you are an objective and therefore compatible prospective employee. You're back with Mr. Big, the man to whom you will report and out of whose budget your salary will come. His mission is to get you for as little as he can, to make the very best buy he can for the company's money. Your job is to sell yourself for the most money possible without being greedy or unrealistic.

Obviously, if the job had a price tag on it or the contemplated salary was disclosed during Phase One, the fact that you're there indicates that the described compensation is satisfactory to you. There is no pay problem. Only when the matter of compensation is open-ended or "negotiable" do you play what is called the "numbers game" with Mr. Big. The object of that game is for you to make him quote numbers first. This takes some devious doing on your part.

Many people are reluctant to play this game, for fear that they will antagonize Mr. Big and perhaps lose the job. But the interview process is not yet over. Further evaluation is still going on. Managers everywhere are constantly negotiating with someone — suppliers, customers, competitors, unions. If you cannot negotiate on your own behalf, it would be unrealistic to expect you to be able to negotiate on behalf of your company or your management. It would be a shame to score badly at this late date, so you've got to hang in hard, you've got to play the "numbers game."

It will start with Mr. Big asking you, "When will you be available?" If you say "Right away" he'll think you're up against it financially, especially if you're unemployed. If you're working, he might feel that your current position is such an abrasive, impossible work situation you'll do anything to escape it. Either way, it will add up to discount in Mr. Big's mind, and influence what happens from here on. It will have a direct bearing on his offer. He also wants to know if you will give your current employers adequate notice. Your "Right away" reply infers that you will walk out, not give decent notice, put the company you are leaving in an awkward position and maybe even in a bad hole. Mr. Big wouldn't want you doing this to him, so he doesn't expect you to do it to your present employers either.

How much notice you have to give will also indicate to Mr. Big where you are in your present hierarchy. Only people low on the totem pole give two weeks notice. Managers have to give at least a month, and frequently more. Mr. Big knows this and is prepared to wait for you. Don't spoil his good impression of you by being overly eager, inconsiderate of your current bosses, or both. Play a little hard to get.

If Mr. Big notes a touch of desperation in your efforts to get out of your present situation, he'll probably only match your current earnings or maybe even offer you a little less. If he feels your situation isn't that bad, that you can tolerate it for some time yet while you conduct a leisurely search for something better, he's going to have to make it worth your while to switch. He wants you, so he's going to have to entice you away with a pay raise, an increase over your current earnings of perhaps 10 to 20 percent.

To help yourself, answer Mr. Big's question with one of your own. When he asks about your availability, respond with "When will you need me?" If he names a date thirty to forty-five days away, the first of a month that is not too close, or right after an upcoming holiday, say, "Fine, I'll be available." But he might say, "Need you! I need you yesterday. Can you start tomorrow?" Maybe you want this job so badly that you will be unable to resist saying yes. If you are employed and answer this way, you may not get the job after all. If you do get it, Mr. Big will never trust you no matter how long you work for him. He'll always be wondering when it will be his turn to have you walk out on him without giving adequate notice.

Be confident that you are doing the right thing, and tell Mr. Big that you won't be able to start for six weeks or two months or whatever. Explain that you're in the middle of a project that you've been in charge of since the very beginning and that it would be an unfair, undeserved hardship on your current company if you were to walk away from things now that they're nearing the climax. You'll come a-running just as soon as matters are buttoned up, which should be in so many weeks or months.

He'll respect you for your concern. He'll want the same consideration extended him should you ever decide to leave him. This conduct will make him want you more than ever, and he'll wait for you. You will again have gotten high marks for your morals, ethics, conscience in matters of timing, seeing things through; even for your plain decency and your sense of courtesy. You won't lose by doing the honorable, right thing. You will lose if you do anything else. You have to remember that everything Mr. Big tells you about his pressing need is not necessarily the truth. He may be baiting you and overstating in an effort to evaluate your character and your ability to resist seduction.

Even if you are unemployed, your cause will not be

helped by jumping eagerly and agreeing to start tomorrow or next week. There are several reasons you should still play hard to get. First of all, Mr. Big has been interviewing a slate of candidates. Out of these six or eight people you may be the only one who is unemployed. All the others will have to give decent notice to their present employers, so Mr. Big knows that the odds are that he is going to have to wait. It is wise to try to stay on the same peer level as the employed candidates.

Don't come on like distress merchandise, a fire-sale bargain, just because you're not working. Instead of matching your old salary level or going a little above it, Mr. Big will offer you a 10 to 20 percent cut from your last earnings level. Remember that Mr. Big is prepared to increase, by that same 10 to 20 percent, the salaries of the employed candidates in order to persuade them to leave their present jobs and join him. So as much as a 40 percent earnings differential is involved here.

Also, keep in mind later in this book you are going to learn the mechanics of marketing yourself. If you apply what you learn, in just a matter of weeks you should have three or four offers from which to choose. If you precipitately bite at Mr. Big's bait, his urgent need for you, whether it be real or not, you're not going to have much of a career. How can you be happy, which is what a career is all about, if you're going to wonder and worry constantly whether you did the right thing? Would you have been better off to have explored the marketplace further? Instead of allowing yourself only one choice, should you have looked more carefully at options and alternatives? Such doubts gnawing away in the back of your mind cannot fail to result in unhappiness and hurt your career. The job you took too early with Mr. Big might have turned out to be the best of the lot. But, you'll never know, because you have no basis for comparison, so you'll go on wondering and second-guessing yourself.

Stall for time for the aforementioned reasons. Come up with an airtight excuse for not being able to start right away. You can't say you're in the midst of painting the house or resodding the lawn. Mr. Big might just say to get in a painter or gardener to finish the job at his expense. Getting you cheap, since you proved you are not a very tough negotiator, he can pay for the painter or gardener and still spend less than his budgetary allocation for the position. So give him an excuse that will hold water, that will stand up to scrutiny and Mr. Big's efforts to knock it out, and don't back down.

Figure out something that fits your circumstances, something along the lines of your being the executor of the estate of a recently deceased out-of-town relative. You have to dispose of a lot of property and make bequests to the other beneficiaries. There's no way you can delegate this duty to anyone else, but you've already started and figure it will take about two more months. Mr. Big can't get nosey, asking who died, where, or how much money is involved. Even if he suspects the excuse is fictional, he's got to admire its ingenuity.

At the same time, you're disabusing Mr. Big of any notion that you're up against it financially. He knows that executors of a will are almost invariably prime beneficiaries also. So you have, or will shortly have, a cushion that will enable you to take your time and be quite selective about your next job. If he really wants you, instead of knocking down the price he'll have to up it to get you. You have brought yourself to the same level as the employed prospects on Mr. Big's slate of candidates.

If at the end of five or six weeks you've looked at other opportunities and none of them is as good as Mr. Big's job, you can always phone him saying you lucked into some fleet sales and got rid of your executor's chores faster than you thought. Instead of starting on the fifteenth as planned, you can come in early, on the first. Mr. Big's reaction will be a happy affirmative, of course. If you call shortly before the fifteenth saying you need two more weeks and can only start the first of the following month, Mr. Big might just tell you to forget it and go to his second choice from among the candidates. It is always easier to advance a deferred starting date than to back it up, so be sure you ask for enough time initially to conduct your other explorations.

Needless to say, all the stall tactics are off if you have been unemployed long enough to be flat broke, with a stack of unpaid bills and the sheriff about to foreclose. In that case, start immediately and get back on your financial feet. After your bills are paid off and you've built up a reserve you can remarket yourself if you are so inclined. You may find that Mr. Big's job is quite a good one, and that you're compatible and content. If so, stay put. There is no utopia out there in the business world, no spot where you're going to be deliriously happy. Happiness results not so much from positive factors as it does from the absence of negative factors like frustrations and abrasiveness. If you can be content where you are doing your thing, that's happiness enough. Looking for too much, the ideal, could amount to chasing rainbows.

At any rate, if you are employed, you can afford to take your time and be highly selective about where you go next. If you are unemployed, all this becomes a judgmental matter. If you can afford it, take your time and be selective. If not, get off the street and become solvent before you readdress yourself to the matter of resuming your career. The fiscal immediacies take priority over longer range considerations.

Having a career is not a happening, with some fairy godmother tapping you with her wand, transforming you overnight into a captain of industry. A career is a planned progression from immediate to intermediate to long-range goals. It may sometimes be necessary to detour temporarily, to accept a less than ideal immediate situation in order to accomplish the intermediate and long-range objectives better. You must decide when you have to detour. The best solution, the long-term answer, might involve a stop-gap, temporary start. You would not be succumbing to subjective expediency; you would be facing reality.

As the first order of Phase Three business, get the starting date disposed of. Come to some understanding with Mr. Big as to when you will come aboard his ship and take over your duties. Hopefully, this date will be deferred. If you can't afford the delay, start at once, even at a lower salary. You can retrieve later. Beyond the monetary considerations, you'll be dealing from a position of greater strength; it is always easier to resituate if you're employed than if you're unemployed. And the longer you're out of work, the harder it becomes.

At your first audience in Phase Two, Mr. Big will learn you left your last company some six months ago. Mr. Big is going to say to himself, "I think he's pretty great, but he's been out of work for six months. Surely during this time he's had quite a few interviews, with none of them successful. I wonder what all the other interviewers saw in him that I've missed." Now there's a question about you. Much will depend on Mr. Big's courage about his own convictions, his judgment. He might elect to go the safe route and pass you by.

However, even if you've been out of work a long time, you should still be able to make yourself irresistible, to reinforce the courage of Mr. Big's convictions, by using the precepts and interview techniques you're learning from this book. He'll say to himself, "I think he's great. I've uncovered a real gem. Sure he's been out of work for a long time and has had a lot of no-result interviews. But he's obviously highly selective. And the other interviewers weren't smart enough to discern what I've found out about him — his great objectivity. Their loss is my gain; on he goes up the referral line."

By the way, proceeding objectively is not just a trick or technique to get you through interviews successfully then to be discarded and forgotten. You've got to follow through as advertised, you must deliver as per your promise. Objectivity must be your on-the-job stance later, your managerial philosophy and approach for the rest of your working life.

With the starting date established, Mr. Big will continue. He will want to know your income expectations, your salary requirements. However he phrases it, it adds up to "How much?" At this point do not reach into your pocket and produce your W2 form from last year. Nor do you quote a figure. He is not trying to buy a $15,000-a-year or even a $25,000-a-year man. If he wants you badly enough, he'll pay what he has to to get you. Part of his job, his responsibility, is to make this as little as possible. Furthermore, he may have another incentive to keep your salary low. He may enjoy a percentage share of the saving he has effected if he runs his department under budget.

You're about to start playing the numbers game with Mr. Big. To do this, you need a basis from which to proceed. You need some facts. Answer his "how much" question with one of your own. "Are you satisfied that I am the man for the job and are you making me an offer, Mr. Big?" Obviously you are not going to get a negative answer from him. You've been back and forth many times, you've seen many people, you're too far down the track for that. You'll get a yes, or at worst a "yes, but." Find out what he still has doubts or reservations about and rebut that but. It may be something that wasn't covered in enough detail earlier, so go back over your background and get rid of his doubts. You've got to get him to say "Yes, we think you're the man for the job."

Now you've got a firm base from which to operate, to establish control. Go on with "I'm glad to hear you say that, Mr. Big. I, too, think I am the man for the job. Now that we've got that most important part of the interview over with, I'm sure we won't have any problem with the matter of compensation. By the way, what's your thinking in this regard?" Mr. Big may quote figures, but it is much more likely that he will not. As a skilled negotiator he will probably bang the ball back to your side of the tennis court, saying, "Our thinking is so fuzzy it is almost meaningless. We've never had your kind of guy aboard before so we have no experience to draw from. You're the old pro who's been doing your thing out there for a long time. What's it going to take to get you?"

You cannot rise to Mr. Big's bait. Return the ball to him. "I can appreciate the fact that you haven't had my kind of guy aboard before, but when you and your group decided to go ahead with this project, you must at least have come up with some cost estimates. What are those?" Mr. Big may give you numbers, but he's much more apt to continue the game. He will continue to evaluate your negotiating skill by replying, "Our estimates are much too open-ended to be meaningful. What we need is help from someone like you — somebody to paint in the base lines and tie down the bags in our ball park. What is that going to cost us?"

You cannot cave in and quote numbers first. Come back at him once more, sympathetically. "I can appreciate your position, Mr. Big, but before you and your group decided to proceed with this project, you must have done considerable research into the matter. What is your competition paying my kind of guy?" Maybe he'll mention a figure. More likely he won't; he'll respond with, "You're right. We did a tremendous amount of research. We know our competition's rack prices and their landed freight costs. We know their sales and advertising costs. We know their raw material costs because we buy from the same sources. We know their labor costs because we use people from the same union. We've got a pretty good handle on everything except a few of the staff jobs in middle management such as yours would be. On these we don't even have an inkling. Come on, help us. Tell us what you're looking for."

Do not respond to his importuning. You've got one last arrow in your quiver, so fit it into your bow and let it fly. "Mr. Big, I'm delighted but not surprised that you did such a thorough research job. This kind of information will be very helpful to me later. Obviously, this is a very well-run business. But in any well-run business, before a project of this kind could be started a budgetary allocation would have to be made. What are your budget figures for my job, Mr. Big?" You can safely bet that there is a budget. And you've maneuvered him to the point where he has to quote a figure first. You've won the numbers game.

You've also passed Mr. Big's evaluation of your negotiating skill. You did not hit him between the eyes by asking the budget question first. That would not be negotiating. It would be bulldozing, coming on like a Sherman tank. Instead, you've led him and set him up so that he has to describe his budget bracket for your position. Obviously, this is what you want to happen. This is why you've played the numbers game. His figures may be considerably higher than what you might have dared to stab at if you had had to say the numbers first. You might have come in and worked just as hard for a lot less money than the company is prepared to pay.

Mr. Big will describe the range. Under $25,000 the usual bracket is a $3,000 spread: $15,000 to $18,000, $18,000 to $20,000, and so on. Over $25,000 the spread usually increases to $5,000: $25,000 to $30,000, $30,000 to $35,000. Over $40,000 the spread broadens to $10,000. If the bracket mentioned is higher than you hoped, do not subside happily and start at the bottom of it. Your negotiating skill is still being evaluated. Only a working stiff down on the line would say, "Whee! Five dollars an hour! I'll take it! Where is the grindstone for my nose?" Besides, why wait a year for a salary review to bring you up to where you might start if you spend five minutes more at this propitious moment while the tide is running your way?

Don't be greedy and try to start at the top of Mr. Big's happily high bracket, although you should try to stay away from the lower end. Don't mention what you need or prefer. Talk about the extras and plusses you are bringing to the job. Show where they go beyond the company's initial expectations and job description, and how the company will be deriving unexpected benefits in which you would like to share. Do your petitioning cerebrally and logically, not emotionally. Let Mr. Big know that you are not looking to start at the top of the range. But because of the extras you bring with you, you simply believe that you deserve better than a start at the bottom end of the bracket. Mr. Big should agree that you're worth more and agree to sweeten the pot by another thousand or two.

At this point, stop. You've accomplished your purpose. You've made your point. You've maintained your managerial credibility and posture. And you have proved again that you know how to negotiate. Also, by stopping in the middle of the bracket, you're letting Mr. Big win a little, too. He'll be saving face. Otherwise, his boss Mr. Big-Big might start to wonder about Mr. Big's negotiating skill if he started you at the top salary possible. Accepting the bottom or shooting greedily for the top would be subjective extremes. As an objective manager you try to reach the middle; once you reach it, you try to stay there. The same philosophy pertains in a salary negotiation.

Suppose Mr. Big mentions a salary bracket below what you're looking for. Don't pack up and leave. Several things could be going on. Mr. Big might still be making a last-ditch effort to get you for as little as possible, and may be understating his budget. He may be coming in low purposely to see how you handle the matter. He may be checking out your naiveté versus your awareness of what goes on in interviews. As a general rule of thumb Mr. Bigs everywhere have a 20 percent upward negotiating latitude from the top of their described bracket. Ordinarily, Mr. Big can raise a stated range of, say, $18,000 to

$20,000, to $24,000 without having to go to his boss, the salary committee, or the executive committee for approval.

You have a sales job on your hands. Go over all the plusses you bring to the job. Say to Mr. Big, "When we began our discussions several days (or weeks) ago you were looking for a man who would give you such and such coverage. We both know that I am very considerably broadening the spread of that coverage. In view of that, it would seem only logical that your compensation spread should be broadened accordingly. The range you mention is a little low and would represent a cut from my past earnings."

Again, don't talk about your wants or needs. Don't say you're a $25,000-a-year man and won't take a penny less. Leave out all emotionality, all subjectivity. Try to convince him that you're worth more because of the additional benefits you are bringing him and his company. Usually this approach will get the desired result. Mr. Big will agree you're worth more and up the ante.

Occasionally Mr. Big will say he's locked into the range he quoted. Check out the fringe benefits. Some firms pay well but give little else. Other firms don't pay as well but offer all kinds of fringe goodies. If you had to field these yourself at your own expense, and after taxes, the job that paid a larger salary might be worth less than the one with the lower base pay. There are no standard packages of fringe benefits.

Don't make up your mind that you won't take the job, and don't give up yet. Find out what else you get before you decide. Otherwise, you'd be guilty of a subjective prejudgment made with only part of the facts in hand. You are not being thorough. You haven't learned all you need to know before making your decision.

Sometimes Mr. Big says he hasn't the authority to go higher but agrees you are worth more money and will take up the matter with his boss. Mr. Big-Big, unfortunately, is out of town and won't be back until next Tuesday. Mr. Big will call you some time about the end of next week. Don't hold still for this "don't call us, we'll call you" bit. Never surrender the recontacting initiative. If you pursue the marketing tactics and strategies you'll shortly be learning here, things could get quite busy. When you relinquish control over follow-ups, you may find yourself behaving like Lonesome Susie, the wallflower who is afraid to leave the phone for fear it will ring while she is gone. Instead, you want to be actively pushing ahead with your marketing campaign, out seeing people, getting audience, and when it is time to recontact someone, doing the phoning from wherever you are.

Get yourself a telephone credit card if you don't already have one. To get one, merely call your local Bell business office. Using such a card will prevent operators from interrupting your conversation for more money. It will be especially convenient for long-distance follow-up calls. You won't have to worry about having lots of change. You could be calling from a phone on the road, where changing bills to silver might be quite difficult to manage. A little objective anticipation can make things a lot easier.

At any rate, tell Mr. Big, "I've got a lot of out-of-town interviews scheduled for next week, so it might be difficult for you to catch me. Rather than inconvenience you that way, here's what I'd like to do. Mr. Big-Big will be back next Tuesday. Let's give him a couple of days to catch up with the accumulation on his desk, and give you a couple of days to catch up with him and discuss the matter. I'll call you sometime next Friday to see what his answer is."

You have demonstrated to Mr. Big that you understand your mission, which is to make things as easy for him as you can. You've also helped him by providing ammunition and a sales argument for him to use on Mr. Big-Big by your casual commentary about other interviews. Mr. Big can say to Mr. Big-Big, "All of us, including you, think he's great. And plenty of other people must think so too because he's got a lot of interviews scheduled. He's looking for more money than we've budgeted. If we want him, and I certainly do, we're going to have to pay him what he's looking for. Otherwise we'll lose him. Another $5,000 should land him. He's too objective a manager for us to let him slip away. Besides, he's giving us a lot more coverage than we were initially hoping for, and we based our present salary range on lower qualifications. I think he's worth the extra money. What do you think?" Mr. Big-Big would probably not refuse his subordinate. Odds are he will okay his request.

It is possible that Mr. Big will gratefully accept your offer to call back but will qualify it. "If you're going to call me Friday make sure it is before 11 A.M., as I'm get-

157

ting an early start on a weekend up at the lake. I'm going to put my boat in the water (or take it out of the water)." Don't ever get tied down to a specific time to call. You may not be able to get to a phone for some reason. Between 9 and 11 A.M. next Friday you could be 30,000 feet over Erie, Pa., flying to an interview in New York. You may not know about the interview yet. It could be set up between now and then.

Mr. Big delays his departure for the lake by twenty minutes, a half hour, forty-five minutes, and still no call from you. Even though he has good news for you, your failure to call is bound to bother him, so it is no way for you to go. Tell him, if he gives you a time limitation, that you expect to be on a plane next Friday morning, that you want to avoid delaying his weekend, and that you'll call him sometime Monday instead. Now that you have all day and a phone credit card, you can call him from anywhere, from either side of the country.

By the way, should the "how much" question come up very early, during Phase One or early in Phase Two, beware! This is a sign that you've flunked and are being busted out. Mr. Big doesn't want to hurt you or get into arguments with you by telling you that you're too subjective, or too strong, or a threat, or abrasive. He'll let you down easy, using money as the excuse. No matter what figure you mention, it will never be right. You'll always be underqualified or overqualified, never on target.

If you don't get the job, try to retrieve something from the situation. Convert this negative into as much of a positive as you can by finding out the real reason.

Maybe whatever it is can be modified, is something you can improve or something you can avoid doing in future interviews. Try to derive some profit, some benefit, from this lost cause.

Ask Mr. Big "Are you satisfied that I am the man for the job and are you making me an offer?" Mr. Big of course will say no. Whereupon you can say "If I'm not the man for the job, what difference does it make how much I'll work for, down to and including nothing? So let's establish first whether or not I am the man for the job. The matter of compensation can wait until that's done." You have smoked out Mr. Big. He'll have to give you the real reason or reasons, or come pretty close. At least, he will no longer be able to use money as the excuse, and hopefully you will learn something about yourself by his perceptions of you that will be of use to you later.

After Mr. Big has given you this help, don't forget to thank him. Don't flounce out in a huff, insulted. Don't tell him off or otherwise burn bridges behind you. He might be of use to you someday, as a customer, as a source, or in some other way. So keep everything low key, and keep your emotions under control. There'll be other opportunities and other interviews for which you'll be better prepared, thanks to what you've just learned. Just keep in mind that there are more fish in the sea than have ever been caught, and carry on your campaign.

Now, let's get back to Phase Three. You've gotten the matter of base pay settled satisfactorily. If not, you're faced with a take it or leave it situation, with a lower base pay than you hoped for. You're now finding out about the rest of the package so that you can make an objective decision on whether or not to accept the offer. Find out what else there is in the way of direct compensation — commission, bonus, profit sharing, override, other financial incentives you may collect quarterly, semi-annually, or annually instead of each pay period. If you operate your department under budget you might receive a percentage of the saving you've effected. If you bring off some coup that is a moneymaker you might get recognition by an immediate raise or a bonus separate from periodic salary reviews. Maybe you get stock options or even an outright gift of some shares. Find out!

Find out what indirect compensation you get. Is there a company-paid membership in a luncheon club, an athletic club, a country club? Do you get a company car, a company gas credit card, a company American Express, Diners, or Carte Blanche credit card, a company air travel card? Are there limitations on your expense account, with everything beyond a certain figure charged to you, or is your expense account unlimited? Do you have to advance your own money as you incur company-related expenses, submitting vouchers for later reimbursement, or do you merely sign, with the company doing the rest, the invoices going directly to it?

Do you get your turn at the company cottage up at the lake? If you and your family can vacation there, that's a considerable saving. If you take graduate work will the company pay for books and tuition? Will it pay for your transportation to, and registration for, seminars you might need to attend to stay abreast of your discipline? If you have to attend conventions on behalf of the company, can you bring your wife along? Would she be at your expense or theirs? There are a lot of women up North who get pretty unhappy about shoveling snow while old Dad is attending week-long conventions in Florida two or three times a winter. See if you can't take her along at company expense. She'll be a lot happier and you'll be less likely to get into trouble.

Next find out about its life insurance policy. Is it participatory or paid for by the company? If participatory, what is your share? Is it portable, or does it terminate when you leave? If the face value of the policy isn't sufficient for your needs can you increase it by paying the additional premium but at the lower, group rate? Do you have continued vestment at face value after retirement, or are there annual percentile decreases until, say at the age of eighty-five, there's barely enough left to bury you? The life insurance you get is very important. Paying for such protection out of your own pocket can be very expensive, with the premiums getting higher as you grow older.

Next find out about hospitalization and health insurance. Do you have a simple Blue Cross-Blue Shield type of policy, with, say, the first $100 deductible and a $10,000 limit per illness? Or do you have a major medical policy that may have the same $100 deductible but provides a $40,000-$50,000 limitation per illness? Do you get an executive medical policy with no deductible and no limitation? Most companies pay for medical insurance without employee participation. Make sure this is the case, as you might run into a rare exception.

As you ask about these indirect benefits, be careful how you do it. Never ask, directly or indirectly, "What are you going to do for me here, and what do I get there?" Instead, say, "What is your policy regarding . . .?" or "What is your company practice with regard to . . ." or "How do you handle . . .?" Don't make your questions sound too personal, too self-oriented. You don't want to seem to be looking for special treatment. You want instead to project interest in how the company treats such matters across the board for everyone in its employ as a matter of standard policy.

If relocation is involved, most companies, but not all, pay moving expenses. Some only pay on an installment basis; you may have to pay the mover, with the company reimbursing you for one-third the expense on your first, second, and third anniversaries. This installment practice began because many big-city companies got tired of moving country boys in from the prairies, with nine rooms of furniture, kids, cats, and canaries, only to have them leave in six months or so. These guys were only looking for a free ride into the big town, with its greater opportunities. They spoiled a good thing by taking unfair advantage of it.

You can help yourself by getting an estimate from a long-distance mover before going on distant-city interviews so that you'll have some idea of the expense involved. Because most such movers are notorious for underestimating, tack on another third; that should come close to what the real cost will be. Also factor in a few hundred dollars for repairs to damaged furniture. There are sure to be some tears, scratches, and broken arms or legs. (You may already have learned that three relocations are equivalent to a fire; your furniture is just about wiped out.)

At any rate, there is little likelihood you will collect full damages from the mover, who in all probability will be self-insured. The usual tactic is to stall. The mover may note damage on the bill of lading at the time of delivery, but then you wait weeks or months for an examiner or adjuster to appear. Eventually one will show up, but in the meantime you've gotten tired of waiting and had the repairs made yourself so that you could utilize the furniture. The examiner, when he arrives, says, "I don't see any scratches on this table," he crosses it off the list, and you are not reimbursed.

There is every likelihood of later hidden expenses as well. After living in the new location for a few months your wife may decide that the old drapes don't fit, that the carpet you brought along isn't the right color for the new house, or that some of your furniture is in the wrong decor since you've moved from a ranch-style to a Georgian-style house. Some things will have to be replaced.

Having done your homework, and armed with at least ball-park moving arithmetic, ask Mr. Big his practice on relocation expenses. He might tell you to have the movers send their invoices to him. But he might say that you pay and are reimbursed in annual installments.

Maybe you don't have that kind of money lying around. Remember, however, that you're still negotiating. Mr. Big's position is probably not rigid. Sometimes a gesture or token of good faith is all that's needed.

Tell Mr. Big, "I certainly want to join your team but moving is going to cost approximately x thousands of dollars, which I don't have. I'd hate to have to turn down the job for that kind of reason so I wonder if we can't work around it some way. For example, if you were to pay the moving expenses we could withhold $100 or $200 from every paycheck and keep it in escrow until the total you laid out has been reached, at which time it would revert to me." If Mr. Big doesn't want to lose you, he'll agree to your suggestion. Incidentally, this could be a fine form of payroll savings for you.

You don't want to pick out your new house all by yourself. The rest of your family might be quite unhappy about your choice. Coming home every night to a bunch of long faces would soon affect you and impair your work effectiveness. Unless your children are very young, it isn't a decision that just you and your wife should make, either. If your kids are of school age they should have a chance to compare neighborhoods and schools. The decision should be made by the total family, by everyone coming with you.

Where you work may be largely your decision as breadwinner, based on how compatible you and the job are. Given that broad prerogative, the neighborhood in which you settle your family is a matter of everyone's compatibility. Try to arrive at a reasonable consensus. If your kids should prove to be somewhat unrealistic, especially about the fiscal end of it, that is understandable and to be expected. You and your spouse will have to provide the realism required.

However, don't impatiently brush off your children's opinions. Try to make them understand why something can't be done or had. Keep in mind that pulling up stakes and moving to a strange city can be a traumatic experience for them, and that if they had a choice they'd probably prefer to stay put. The decision to go was not theirs. Don't make matters worse by excluding them further and by being totally arbitrary in all matters, especially those in which they can and should be given some voice. Otherwise, they may become so negatively preconditioned that they'll never adjust to the new surroundings. If that happens everyone will end up unhappy.

Mr. Big understands these circumstances and recognizes the need for family compatibility. If he's paying relocation expenses, he will include some front money for exploration purposes. He'll bring in your family, but the question is, for how long? If you and your family are looking over the area on your own, you might need as much as three or four weeks for comparison purposes. During this time you may be working. If so, your family will have to do the initial looking and screening. You will only participate nights and weekends, narrowing down the options.

Meanwhile, put yourselves up in a moderate-priced motel or hotel, of the Howard Johnson's or Holiday Inn type. Eat from the middle of the menu. Those places not only have reasonably priced daily specials, the specials are usually their chief claim to culinary fame. Don't put yourself up at the Ritz Towers and eat Chateaubriand every night. On the other hand, don't hide away at the Nighty-Night Motel and live on McDonald hamburgers. Both courses are extreme, so stay away from them.

Mr. Big may give you two or three weeks or a month in which to settle down somewhere. He may leave the term open-ended. Try to find a place within the stated period. If you run a few days over you might be better advised to pay for the overtime yourself. If he is paying "until," don't loaf. Get the matter finished as quickly as you can, consistent with thoroughness.

If Mr. Big's term is too short for you to relocate properly, take advantage of stop-gap alternatives. Rent a house for a year with an option to buy even though it may not be everything you want. Rent an apartment. With a base of operation you can conduct a more leisurely exploration of better locations, and find the one at which you can put down roots later. The temporary solution will prevent you from wearing out your welcome with Mr. Big. You will have gotten yourself and your brood off his back and out of his budget.

See if it is Mr. Big's practice to provide relocation help of any kind. Some firms relocate so many people they've been forced into the real estate business and have personnel or even whole departments handling such matters. Short of that, Mr. Big might be able to refer you to some real estate agents and to banks or savings and loan associations for mortgages. He might even know about some appropriate houses that are not listed. Out of concern for neighbors and neighborhoods, many owners who are willing to sell will not make this knowledge public but instead will proceed confidentially on a principals-only referral basis. This way also saves agents' fees and commissions for both buyer and seller.

One last point to keep in mind about relocating is that you may be leaving a house on which you have an old mortgage at, say, 5.5 or 6.5 percent. To buy an equivalent house will cost a lot more today, and your mortgage rate will probably be 8.5 to 9.5 percent, with points tacked on besides. This additional expense could wipe out a big chunk of your salary increment. Many companies are aware of this, and provide help against this kind of hidden loss by cost-of-mortgage-differential allowances. These allowances are frequently treated as a business operation expense rather than part of its payment for services. If you fall into this loss category, find out if Mr. Big and his company do anything about such situations. Even if they just split the difference with you, that would be of some help.

Inquire only if the mortgage will work a real hardship on you. If you're making a big profit on the sale of your old house, the one you're buying isn't that much more expensive and the mortgage differential isn't that great, forget it. Don't be greedy and try to extract every last dollar from the company. It is making an investment in you. If it recognizes that you are reciprocating in kind, that you are not trying to go down the one-way street of taking but never giving, if it sees you making some investment of your own in the position, it's going to feel a lot better about you, your intentions, and your motivations. Most of the other Phase Three negotiation matters will be less open-ended and more fixed. Relocation will be the most flexible. Get it settled and out of the way with a minimum of haggling.

Undesirable Hiring Conditions

Now that you have all the particulars, make up your mind what you want to do about such matters as going to Weeweehootchie later. Maybe the entire deal shapes up in such fine fashion that you decide not to bring up the subject, that you'll accept the Weeweehootchie condition. If you think your arrangement isn't that great, or that you still can't or don't want to go to Weeweehootchie, now is the time to discuss it and to try to get it removed as a hiring consideration.

Just as you were objectively thorough in waiting to learn the total compensation package before making your decision, you must continue objectively if you've decided that you won't go to Weeweehootchie. Hopefully, you've given the matter some thought, running over in your mind what you're going to say on the subject.

You can't make it sound as if it's only a personal bias that is stopping you. The reasons have to be objective, and as generic as possible. "One of my children has an unusual health problem. The prognosis is good that it can be cured in time, although nobody can predict how long it will take. Meanwhile, he has to have special treatment two or three times a week. This therapy can only be administered by a handful of the very biggest hospitals in the country, and none of them is in or even near Weeweehootchie. Maybe he'll be cured before Weeweehootchie time but we can't count on that. If he is still undergoing therapy I won't be able to go. With that understood, and if it is okay with you, I'd still like to join your team. Maybe when the time comes we can work out some other arrangement."

Another suitable reason might be "We have a bit of a problem that may or may not come up. My mother is in a nursing home just a few blocks from where we live. She's eighty, blind, and in a wheelchair, and requires a lot of professional attention we can't give her at home. The only thing that seems to keep her alive is our visits. Someone in the family sees her every day, with everybody taking turns. Since we can continue to live where we are while I'm revising the graphics and conducting the distributor salesmen seminars, it is not an immediate problem. But if she is still alive when it comes time to transfer to Weeweehootchie, we won't be able to go. We're all the family she has, and she can't be moved, according to her doctors, so maybe some other arrangement can be worked out then to everyone's satisfaction. With that understood, I'd very much like to come aboard."

Or you could say "My three children are champion skiers, all of whom have won state and regional age-group medals in slalom and downhill. They came by their interest through my younger brother, who was a medalist in the '68 Winter Olympics. Since he lives right in town he's been coaching my children on the slopes where he works. He thinks that in four or five years they'll be Olympic qualifiers and winners. Meanwhile, the kids are deadly serious and dedicate many long hours of daily practice toward that Olympic goal. For the next couple of years everything would be okay, while I revise the graphics and conduct distributor salesmen seminars from my present home. But comes time to go to Weeweehootchie, I don't know if I'll be able to rip the kids away from ski country. It would just about break their hearts.

"Once before, with my present company, I had a chance to relocate to the South. When they heard about it, all the ski people got into the act, talking about duty and patriotism. Everything considered I didn't have the heart to proceed. I just could not disregard everything and everybody else, especially my kids, for the sake of my own advancement. Since it happened before, it'll happen again, only more so. I'll probably not make the Weeweehootchie move then, either, because of having to keep my family in snow country. Is there any way we can work around this? I'd love to join your team."

In any of the foregoing instances, if Mr. Big says it's Weeweehootchie or else, don't take the job. However, he may compromise or even eliminate that condition, or he may defer his decision until the time comes in the hope that your son will have been cured or your mother will have passed on. Since he knows you have reservations about Weeweehootchie, if he still invites you aboard the onus is off you and you can accept the offer in good conscience.

Letter of Confirmation

Having agreed to all terms and conditions, you are shaking hands with Mr. Big and saying good-bye until whenever it is you are slated to report for work. At this point you have one last thing to do. Ask Mr. Big when you may expect his letter of confirmation. A direct question, "When may I expect your letter of confirmation?" will accomplish much. It will let Mr. Big know that you completely understand the whole process you've been through.

Contracts are rarely used these days except in instances of long-deferred pay arrangements that will continue after you've left the company at the end of the contract term. Contracts were always too full of legal terminology, too slanted toward the company, and too full of restrictive covenanting. No court of law was likely to find for the company, thereby depriving some employee of his right to livelihood, to support his family. So contracts were generally superseded years ago by letters of intent. These were not legally binding instruments either, so neither side had any recourse. Like contracts, though, letters of intent were full of legalese "whereases" and "parties of the first and second parts" because they were drawn up by lawyers. In time the awkwardness and cost of letters of intent were recognized, and they, too, fell into disuse.

Today, a company writes an ordinary letter in duplicate on its own letterhead stationery spelling out all the

171

particulars discussed during Phase Three of the interview. The recipient or successful candidate signs the duplicate and returns it to the company, keeping the original for his files. Until you receive this letter of confirmation you have nothing. Even though you have been made a verbal offer, don't go home and start packing.

As has been stated earlier, you are part of a slate of candidates. But you don't know where you appear in that group. Are you one of the early ones, are you in the middle, or are you at the end of the slate? How are they handling that slate — in ascending or descending order of priority? Are they seeing the ones they deem best qualified first, working down the list to the least qualified? Are they going the other way, saving the best for last?

Making you a verbal offer is not dirty pool or a sleazy practice. They're letting you know you're a finalist, and under strong consideration because you're the best they've seen so far. However, they still have other candidates to interview, and one of them might shape up as better than you. If that happens, you won't get a letter of confirmation. Instead, you'll get a letter withdrawing the verbal offer.

You need to know where you are on the slate and how many more guys they'll be interviewing. You also need to know how fast they're proceeding with the process. Are they in a big hurry and dropping everything else to get the job filled? Or are they proceeding in leisurely fashion? Are they so busy keeping up with getting out the wash that they have time to interview only one person a week? If that's the case and they have eight candidates scheduled, of which you were the first, you'll have at least a two-month wait before you can expect the letter of confirmation. If you don't know this you'll have your sweat socks on the whole time, wondering what happened, why you aren't hearing from them, and whether you should follow up. You might even mount a useless follow-up campaign and make a pest of yourself, all because you were not knowledgeable enough to help yourself (and Mr. Big) by asking the simple question, "When may I expect your letter of confirmation?"

When Mr. Big hears this from you he knows you know he's been looking at a slate of candidates, just as you know he knows you've been looking at other jobs. He also knows there is a possibility you may send him a letter withdrawing as a candidate if you find something better between now and starting time. He is aware that you realize you may get a letter withdrawing his offer instead of a letter of confirmation if he finds someone he considers to be better.

Your question clears the air. Now Mr. Big can freely tell you, "We're looking at the best first, and on paper at least you seemed best. But we've got seven guys to go at a one-a-week rate so it will be two months before you hear." He might say, "We only have two to go and they're both coming in next week, so you should hear week after next," or "We went in ascending order, seeing the better men last. You were the last in because you seemed the best on paper. And you proved to be the best in person. So you can take your letter of confirmation home with you, or I'll put it in the mail tomorrow."

You now have a better idea of where you stand. You won't have to wonder, to worry, to follow up. You'll know when you can expect your letter of confirmation if you stand up as best right through the last candidate. You'll also be better prepared to receive a letter withdrawing the offer. You won't go into a state of shock if they find somebody better than you. Obviously, the fewer guys scheduled after you, the less likely you are to be bumped. And the earlier you were, the greater the odds are that you won't be the final choice, unless they went in descending order with the best seen first.

Even if you get a letter of withdrawal, all is not necessarily irretrievably lost. Mr. Big might write how great it was getting to know you during your various visits and how well you qualified for their job as kumquat-dicer. Unfortunately, in the later slate of candidates there was a guy almost your equivalent who lives right in their backyard. Since they didn't have to uproot and relocate him and his family as they would you, they decided to hire him. They'll keep your name on file just in case, and good luck with your search.

Mr. Big showed concern for total family compatibility when he interviewed you, so this reason should not shock or surprise you. A company situated in the South will try to fill its openings with Southerners rather than bring down Midwesterners or New Englanders. There's less adjustment to make to the different mores and lifestyles. You might be quite cosmopolitan and so adapt easily, but what about your family? Similarly, Midwest and New England companies will look to their own regions for help rather than going outside. A small-town company will try to find small-town people rather than bring in someone from New York or Chicago. And a company situated in New York City is not likely to bring in a family from Dry Gulch, Montana, nor will a small company in a small Montana town bring in a Manhattanite and his family. Compatibility would be of concern to the company, and no matter how flexible the candidate might be, complete adaptation might be too much to expect.

If the distance factor did you in, don't despair. In fact, you may have been done a favor. There could have been a serious adjustment problem for you and your family. Go on looking for other opportunities. In a week or two, you may still get a phone call from Mr. Big. He tells you that unknown to him the local man they hired had been hoping to relocate in sun country. In the course of further search he found what he wanted and so withdrew as a candidate for Mr. Big's job. Since you were the equivalent to this man, and the only reason they chose him was his proximity, are you still interested and available? If so, let him know.

If you have had better offers and are no longer interested, tell him. If you have had other offers where long-range prospects aren't as good but the starting pay or perquisites are better, mention only the latter. It may act as leverage for Mr. Big to match or better your other deal, or at least to meet it partway. You can then decide what you want to do.

By the same token, if you uncover a better deal anytime after you've agreed verbally to take another job, even after you've received your letter of confirmation and have signed and returned the duplicate, you can still withdraw as a candidate. You are only officially aboard when you show up at the agreed starting time, hang up your hat and coat, and sign your insurance papers and W4 form. If you disqualify yourself, Mr. Big will contact his second choice.

In most interview situations, to avoid the trouble and expense of having to go through repeat motions, three finalists will be chosen from the slate. Any of these men is considered adequate. Naturally, they'll try to bring in the best first. Failing that, they'll drop to second best, and then to third. If they aren't successful with any of these three, they'll probably restart the whole procedure and bring in a whole new slate by running their ad again or repeating whatever process they used the first time.

If you withdraw as a candidate or they withdraw their offer, nobody can retaliate in any way. Such occurrences are accepted as reality, as a fact of business life. As there is no recourse, it would be pointless for anyone to seek it. Each of you knows that theirs isn't the only basket for your egg and yours is not the only egg for their basket. Don't go into shock if a job you expected goes to somebody else.

And don't get hung up on ethical considerations if you receive a better offer after you've agreed to start somewhere. Take the better offer, of course, and withdraw from the other. Those things go on all the time. It is not dirty pool. It is a recognized objective fact of business reality, so don't be taken advantage of because you are unrealistic. Companies will continue to make their way, with or without you. Nobody is indispensable and nobody is unique.

You are a valuable, viable commodity, and presumably have a lot of career opportunities from which to choose. Explore your options, and do what seems best to accomplish your long-range career objectives. Do not be diverted by somebody else's need for you, a need that may not be in your best interest or coincide with your own goals. Your career is your worry, your problem. You will not solve this problem best by letting yourself be cajoled into solving someone else's problem instead of your own, simply because you committed yourself, gave your word.

Just remember that should a better resolution to the company's problem come along, it would be very quick to get rid of you and absolve itself of its commitment to you. In the interval before you officially start, some member of the board of that company may learn of the opening you expect to fill. He has a nephew who is qualified, not nearly as well as you, but who is looking, so the board member intercedes. You can easily guess what is going to happen to you and your candidacy, despite the letter of confirmation you received, signed, and returned.

Even though a letter of confirmation is not irrevocable and final, it is the best you can hope for. It means the company has stopped its search, gone through the full slate of candidates, and judged you the best man for the job. Barring intercessions from board members with questing nephews or some other internal exercise of clout to disrupt the normal procedure, which is unlikely, you can confidently expect to be hired and can start packing.

Letters of confirmation must be detailed and explicit. Do not sign and return the duplicate of a letter that says, "It was great getting to know you through your various visits. This confirms that you are to start as our head kumquat-dicer on such and such a date at such and such a salary. All the other benefits will be as discussed. We're looking forward to your coming aboard." Memories vary and recollections differ. You don't want to get into a juvenile confrontation later, with a "You said this" or "You promised that," answered by an "I did not."

If the letter of confirmation you receive does not spell out every detail, do not sign it. Instead, write all the terms out as you recall them, and send your own letter to them. Let them sign the duplicate and return it to you, keeping the original for their file. Regardless of who does it or where it originates, there must be a written record of your verbal agreement to avoid possible problems later. Anything less would be unprofessional, unanticipatory, and unwise. Be thorough now and avoid potential problems later that could result from differences in understanding and recollection.

You've sold yourself to a buyer. You've bought a potential career. Make sure the terms of sale, both ways, are spelled out and confirmed by somebody. If the company doesn't do it, you must. You're making a long-term commitment, maybe even for the rest of your working life, so don't be lax and don't treat the matter lightly. Nail it down!

The same pertains if you run into someone who balks at sending a letter of confirmation or gives you the "My word is my bond, sir" bit. Don't argue the point and don't expect the letter. Instead, take the writing initiative and send the letter of confirmation in duplicate to him. Start it off by saying, "The matters we discussed at our last meeting are too important to entrust to memory, since memories can be faulty. In the interest of objectivity and to avoid any future problems, I've confirmed below the details of our conversation as I recall them. If these coincide with your recollections, please sign and return the duplicate for my file, and retain the original for your records."

List everything you've agreed on, dotting every "i" and crossing every "t" and omitting nothing. If he signs and sends back the duplicate, you're fine. If he doesn't, you've got to follow up with a phone call mentioning that you haven't received the letter of confirmation. Maybe he hasn't signed and sent it yet because he hasn't completed going through his slate. Maybe he repeats "I gave you my word. You've got the job. We don't need to sign any letters." You've gotten a verbal confirmation that you're the man for the job, but if the man you're going to be working for is so rigid and unreasonably subjective, maybe you'd better reconsider accepting. Compatibility may be bad.

At least you have one plus going for you if you do accept. He did not take issue with any of the details contained in your letter, which means he has tacitly accepted and approved them. Even though he did not sign it, you have your copy of the letter to use as reference or resource in case you need to. An unconfirmed letter of confirmation is better than nothing. Someplace, in your files or his, there must be a written record of what transpired. If you rely only on what was said, you're asking for trouble, and in all probability you'll get it. You won't win, as your boss is in the dealer's seat, it's his deck, and he's got not only all the aces, but all the other cards as well. He might even ask you to cash in your chips and leave the game.

So, that's what the interview is all about. After asking Mr. Big when you can expect his letter of confirmation, leave. If you're being driven back to the airport by a chauffeur, remember you're still on stage. You can still blow the whole bit by letting your hair down, relaxing, maybe even behaving badly or irresponsibly. If that happens you'll never get your letter of confirmation. Until you have it, you don't want to take one false step. Watch yourself on the way out as much as you did up to this point. The interview is going on as long as you are within sight or hearing distance of anyone in the employ of that company. It did not end when you left Mr. Big's office with an offer.

Personal Portfolio

Many things of legitimate concern to an interviewer are very difficult to ask and equally hard to answer. Mr. Big is concerned about your lifestyle, how you conduct yourself off the job. You may be the soul of decorum while at work, but so far out in your private life that you are a potential source of embarrassment. Mr. Big certainly doesn't want to go around apologizing for the behavior of his subordinates, so he'd like some idea of your social acceptability. You can help him with a few simple snapshots, preferably in color. We don't want contrived pictures, Fabian Bachrach portraiture.

Photographs

Start with your car. If you have children, show the boys getting in or out of the car. We don't want them proudly pointing to the Rolls Royce bonnet or the Cadillac Vee, or doing anything else of an ostentatious nature. We just want Mr. Big to see that you use conventional four-wheel transportation; that you don't go bucketing around on a Honda, a bike, a horse, or a drag-strip racer.

Take a snap of your daughters on the lawn, with your house showing in the background. This is not intended to be some real estate agent's pictorial sales presentation of your property. You're not trying to generate prospective buyer interest. You merely want to show Mr. Big that you live in a conventional dwelling, that you don't live in a hut, a tent, a camper, a trailer, or a bomb shelter. Show a photo of your wife in your living room, with some of your furniture, lamps, and drapes in the background. Mr. Big will be able to see that you have a home; it is not a pad with wall-to-wall mattresses and a few orange crates for furniture.

Three such snaps are all you need. Photos of you are not necessary; they can see you. If you have no children, take pictures of your wife at the car, outside the house, and inside. If you're single, you'll have to be the subject. Have some friend take the same three pictures of you. If you have older children who are grown and gone, don't bother about them. Include only those children who are still at home and will be coming with you if relocation is involved. If all your offspring have left the nest, revert to the three snapshots of your wife.

These photos will comprise the first of five sections making up your portfolio. It will be housed in a three-ring binder that can go to a one-inch thickness in letter-size oversize. The binder should be black, in leather or coriaceous plastic, with a pebbled or scotch-grain finish.

Smooth finishes quickly show smudges and grubby fin-ger marks. Get a dozen or so pliofilm sleeves to put in the binder, plus some attachable tabs for indexing purposes. Instead of running the binder posts through the portfolio contents, we want the contents to be free, so they can be slipped in and out of the sleeves. We're trying to demon-strate again that we know our mission, which is to make things as easy as possible for Mr. Big. If he wants to read the second pages of some portfolio contents, he won't have to fight to disengage the binder posts. Instead, he can slip them out of the pliofilm sleeves, which are all the binder posts go through. The binder's extra half-inch above letter-size width, nine inches instead of eight and a half inches, makes this possible.

Academic Record

The second section consists of all your credentials from academe — degrees, diplomas, certifications of com-pletion, and so forth. Never use originals. They might be difficult to replace, and portfolios have been known to get lost. Use only photocopies of everything in this and the later sections. The photocopies of your educational ac-complishments again make things easier for Mr. Big. He won't have to write and verify.

Mr. Big might be in a hurry to finish deciding who the man for his job is because he has other pressing mat-ters to attend to. He's narrowed his slate of candidates to you and two other people, and it is pretty much a toss-up among you. The other two men have stated their educa-tion and degrees on their résumés or elsewhere, but they would still have to be checked out. You've brought proof with you. Besides the fact that you look more professional, prepared, and aware, you've saved Mr. Big some work. If you were Mr. Big, harrassed and hurried, who would you pick? Touches like this could tip things your way in case of a tie.

Mr. Big is aware that the data most falsified on résumés is not age, contrary to what you might think. It is education, especially from applicants who do not have degrees. One semester gets stretched out to three years, and so on. Some men have been known to research out defunct colleges and purport to have gotten a degree from one. "I got a B.S. in marketing from Siwash in '60. As you know they shut down in 1965. My house burned down in '70, and everything went up in smoke, including my sheepskin, so there's no way I can get a transcript or otherwise prove it. You have to believe me, Mr. Big. I did get a B.S. in marketing from Siwash." You don't have to plead with Mr. Big to take your unsupported word. You don't require him to check. You've shown him photocopy proof. You've made things easier for him.

Military Record

The third section consists of your military record, if any. Show a photocopy of your discharge. Presumably it was an honorable discharge, not a general discharge or a section eight. If you had a commission, show that. Include any citations or commending letters from commanding officers. If you graduated from any military schools while in service, show photocopies of certificates of completion or other proof, such as travel or other orders.

Civic Activities

The fourth section deals with what you've done as a person, preferably of a civic or community nature — membership in or work with the Lions, Kiwanis, Boy Scouts, Little League, PTA, etc. You may have been a member of a board, council, or group. You may have chaired the town's annual clambake, the country club's greens committee, or the town's centennial celebration of its founding. Any recognition of your leadership by your peers will do. Make photocopies of anything you have to support such recognition. Proof could take the form of newspaper articles or photographs, letterheads or program journals bearing your name, thank you letters, anything in print. If you are part of a group photograph, draw an arrow to yourself. If your name is buried in a text, underline it. If what you're exhibiting is difficult to decipher, explain it in a caption. Again, we are trying to make things as easy as we can for Mr. Big.

Professional Activities

The fifth section is concerned with the recognition you have received as a professional. It might be a mention in house organs or trade publications. Photocopy sweetheart letters you may have gotten from clients, associates, or superiors. There may be newspaper articles or photographs. If you have chaired a forum or have been a panelist, a member of an industry committee, or a section head for a Chamber of Commerce, show photocopies of the coverage of such activities. If any of this support material is not clear, draw an arrow, underline, caption, explain.

The inside back cover of most binders has a slash pocket. Carry photocopies of the various letters of recommendation you've accumulated in it. Staple them together into a sheaf, and when you're asked for references, offer the sheaf. Do not volunteer it. References are not as popular as they once were. Obviously, people are not going to give the name of any person who might speak ill of them for a reference. Most references make it sound as if you've taken the Boy Scout oath. Consequently, they're meaningless.

In case you are asked for references, be prepared. It will make it easier for Mr. Big, and easier on your friends. They won't have to repeat their references on your behalf to the point of annoyance. If you don't have reference letters from friends and former employers, get them. Tell these people you're asking them to write a one-time "To Whom It May Concern." Be professional, and have photocopies of the letters ready.

Organization of Materials

Some of us are better pack rats than others. Others may not have bothered saving the kinds of memorabilia that would make up sections 4 and 5. Some may even have been careless about the things making up sections 2 and 3. If that describes you, do the best you can with what you have.

If you've been a head honcho in a number of civic or professional groups but have no printed proof, type up a list of the titles anyway, and describe briefly your responsibilities and what you did over what time span. From now on collect such material in an organized fashion. Get yourself a red-fiber envelope with flap and string that will hold your portfolio. As you accumulate clippings and other things, put them into that envelope for periodic updating. The reason so much valuable material is lost is that it gets thrown into a bureau drawer or secretary, and the kids find it and scribble on it or the dog chews it up. Aside from the help such materials can provide your business career, the portfolio could prove to be a most interesting legacy after you're gone.

If you're newly started in business and don't have much of a track record yet or much proof of accomplishments and recognition, be sure to start accumulating such evidence for later use.

Right now, if all you can come up with are the three snapshots and your education papers, don't put them into a portfolio. Carry the material in your wallet or inside jacket pocket. Otherwise it might appear to be a case of the mountain laboring and bringing forth a mouse.

If you've been in business for some years and have little in the way of personal or professional accomplishments and recognitions, skip the portfolio. You'd look pretty bad showing an emaciated three- or four-page portfolio that said, "This is my life!" You'd be better off without it for now. But get active somewhere, and start accumulating these kinds of data and proofs. As in the case above, you can bring along your three snapshots, the photocopy of your degree, and copies of your reference letters.

If you've been a real tinfoil and string saver all your life and have amassed great volumes of sections 4 and 5 material on yourself, you've got to start eliminating. A manageable portfolio would have between eight and fourteen pages in it, covered on two sides. Anything more would be too much; anything less, too little. You can't hand Mr. Big something of telephone directory thickness; he'll never read it. You wouldn't want him to. It would be too distracting and time consuming. The portfolio is intended to be a visual sales aid for you, a supplement, not a silent-salesman substitute, something you shove into Mr. Big's hands and sit and watch him read.

Use moderation in preparing your portfolio contents. Don't concentrate on any one area. You might have a trunkful of material attesting to your activities in something like the American Legion, culminating in your becoming state commander and a candidate for national office. Mr. Big might wonder which is going to be your career—his company or the Legion. He might not relish your being away a lot, convening, giving speeches, and using up physical and mental energy, and time, on Legion matters. Don't stress that kind of involvement in your portfolio by going on for page after page. Hold things down to several references.

The same pertains for any other outside activity, like your church. You may be Sunday-school superintendent, choir member, president of the men's brotherhood, and church treasurer combined, with a lot of documentary support and proof. In Mr. Big's view you may seem too involved, especially if he only attends church in desultory fashion or is of a different faith.

Once you've left the area of objective moderation, Mr. Big may wonder just how far out you'll go. Are you a frustrated evangelist? A lay preacher? Are you going to spend your lunch hours on a soapbox in a nearby public square, exhorting passers-by to repent and reform? Obviously, he'd want no part of this kind of behavior, so play down any really heavy personal involvements you have. Don't give him cause to worry about immoderation of any sort on your part. He's hoping you'll be compatible off the job as well as on it, and to him compatibility is synonymous with staying in the middle.

Take your portfolio with you as you get audience. Remove it from your attaché case and keep it unobtrusively alongside you in your chair or on your lap. You want it to be instantly available. You do not want to be fumbling with locks, snaps, catches, or zippers trying to get at it, as that would indicate a lack of preparation and anticipation on your part. With your portfolio at the ready, there will be many opportunities for you to introduce it into the proceedings.

Once it is in Mr. Big's hands and you have opened it to the appropriate section, Mr. Big will read the pertinent material. But he will also browse and read the rest, fore and aft of what you've shown him — if the contents are not too lengthy. He'll get a lot of information about your lifestyle, and proof of many things he'd have to check out otherwise. He'll be reading, not hearing from you, what other people think of you. He'll see where you've been and what you've done, and the recognitions you have received. Aside from the great difference in credibility between hearing and reading about something, you now have various associates — not you — saying how great you are. This is a far more acceptable approach. It greatly diminishes the possibility that you will say, "How great I am" too often, and be perceived as self-centered and subjective.

One last word of caution: Do not leave your portfolio with anybody. If Mr. Big has a special interest in some of the contents, his secretary can make copies. If you leave your portfolio with Mr. Big you'll be handicapped at other interviews while you wait to get it back. You want it with you at all times as you talk to people. By perverse fate, the times you don't have it will probably be the occasions you need it most, or could have used it to best advantage. Not leaving your portfolio anywhere will also diminish the chances of its getting mislaid or lost. Put a portfolio together now, or start gathering materials for it if you haven't done enough to fill one at this point. Many men have learned, after being on the job a while, that the difference, the reason they were chosen, was their portfolio. Other candidates who were equally good lacked a portfolio and lost out.

Mechanics of Marketing Yourself

The Bureau of Statistics of the U.S. Department of Labor has been publishing annual figures for some years about placement activity at the executive level. For want of more definitive criteria, such as function, title, or number of subordinates, they broadly peg executive level at the $15,000 or higher salary level. According to their statistics there is an annual 20 percent turnover or 100 percent in five years. In other words, the average tenure on the job is five years.

Average, of course, is a myth. It is made up of a lot of disparate figures. The usual thirty-year-old is still questing, seeking, and going the trial-and-error route; he changes jobs at shorter intervals. The switching usually slows up as a man grows older, many times because he has found what he has been looking for and is content to stay put. An older man of fifty or fifty-five will probably stay where he is until retirement, to finish out his career, so he weights out the average. Maybe he's content, maybe not, but he makes do because he figures it is too late and he's too old to make a change.

AGE

It is not unusual these days for men of twenty-five to be making $15,000 a year. Between the ages of twenty-five and sixty-five there is a forty-year span, and there will always be exceptions to any generalizations that might be made about any of the age groups within this spread. But Mr. Big is aware of the averages. He knows that the younger you are the less likely he is to keep you. He might invest in you, train you, and bring you along; then when he is about to realize a return on his investment, you've gone off to greener pastures. If you're youthful, try to project stability, the idea that you're not just sampling around, that you know what you want to do where and for whom. Make Mr. Big feel that the position he has open is your chosen start on a lifelong career. Don't let him think he's just a way station on your experimental tour, even if it's true.

Companies are recognizing the transience of younger men and what this means in the way of repeat training time and investment expense. They are a lot less gung-ho than they used to be about the youth movement and bringing in whizz kids. These days, hiring older and more experienced men means a lot less training and investment. Ordinarily, such men will become productive quicker, so that a profit can be made from their efforts sooner. Add in the greater stability and retention factors, the greater mileage they'll be getting for less investment, and it is understandable why companies today are being highly selective regarding the recruitment of young men.

Unless the raw employee is really unusual, the company will be getting more for its long-range hiring dollar by taking on an older man. A $20,000 investment in a young man who stays two years or less can net out as a big loss. A $10,000 investment in an older man who stays for fifteen or twenty years is good business. Readers who are over forty should keep these figures in mind. The tide has turned, and is running your way as never before. If you can demonstrate objectivity and flexibility, you'll be welcome a lot of places you were not before.

Stay away from king-size companies; they still won't want you. They continue to prefer youth who can be trained and developed their way. They recognize the heavy attrition and turnover factor, but accept it and calculate it into their costs. Molding "greenies" their way, which is highly structured, is easier in their view, and less costly, than bringing in trained older men. They rather arbitrarily view other experience and training as bad habits that will have to be overcome before their way of doing things can be taught. They also feel that many times these earlier bad habits can't be unlearned; they're too ingrained. But men over forty can try companies below the Fortune 500 size with a reasonable expectation of good interest and reception. Apply what you've been learning here, and you should get interviews and offers.

PLACEMENT OPPORTUNITIES

Another interesting statistic from the Department of Labor is that only 20 percent of the placements come about from openings made public knowledge. This includes listings with search firms and employment agencies, as well as recruitment by newspaper or trade-periodical advertising. Eighty percent of the people hired learned of the opening through someone they knew. A businessman who is not in professional placement knows of an upcoming opening and of a person who has become available and matches them up. He brings job and candidate together successfully. It is this 80 percent of the action we want to address. We'll pay attention to the tip of the iceberg, but we want to concentrate on the greater part of the potential which is below the water line. Where is this 80 percent, and how do we tap it?

Most people tend to socialize and relate with people on their own economic level rather than with people in the same discipline. Engineers don't confine themselves to other engineers. They associate with people who have the same recreational or social interests they do. A further common denominator is that they can afford the same activities, regardless of how they come by the needed loot.

A typical case in point is a country club. Its membership would be quite diverse. It would consist of doctors, dentists, lawyers, bankers, brokers, educators, and a considerable cross section of all kinds of industrialists and businessmen, including the local Buick dealer. All have in common an interest in golf, the fresh air, and the exercise. They also feel the need to relate to a peer group and have the financial capability to maintain membership.

Within this broad framework of hundreds of members, smaller groups will gravitate together in more manageable numbers for further recreational and social purposes. The smaller groups will entertain one another at their homes. They will have cocktail parties, dinner parties, bridge parties, poker parties, and patio barbecues. At all such gatherings, at the club or away, there is a lot of conversation, of course. Nobody ever talks about what he does for a living; that is bad form. The lawyer doesn't discuss the brief he is to present in court tomorrow. The doctor doesn't talk about the frontal lobotomy he is about to perform. The merchant doesn't talk about how good or bad his business is. What do they talk about? They talk about people. They all have people problems and problem people among their clients, patients, students, subordinates, or customers.

Let's construct a hypothetical example of an exchange of confidential placement information. A foursome has finished their regular Saturday morning golf round. They've had the same starting time for years. They're now at the nineteenth hole at a table for a drink or two and some lunch. One of the foursome, whom we'll call Joe, says, "Partner, I feel I ought to pay your Nassau today. We lost both sides and overall, and it was all my fault. I missed a half-dozen putts each side that I ordinarily would have made. My nerves got in the way.

"I've got this guy Jim Jones working for me as a plant manager. You know him. He's not a club member but you've met him around town. Jim has a lot of talent, but he is a minimal performer. He never does any more than he has to do to keep his nose above water, and this drives me up the walls. I'm much too busy with other, more important things to mount a campaign to find a replacement for him. That'll have to wait until early next year, when I have the time. Meanwhile, I'm hoping for a lucky break, for some guy to come wandering through my door before then who can do everything Jones does, and does more of it. When that day comes, Jim Jones goes."

The other three men open their mental file drawers and make an insertion. "Good old Joe needs a plant manager replacement for Jones." They will keep this confidential information actively in mind, as they'd like to be the means whereby friend Joe's problem is solved.

At this point Joe's long-time partner Al, who is in food processing, says, "Joe, you beat me to the punch. I was about to make the same offer to pay your Nassau. As you probably noticed, I yipped more than my share of putts out there today, too. And, for the same reason — nerves. As you know, I've been working as number two man to old man Mose for many years now, expecting to succeed him as president when he retires. Yesterday I got bad news. Mose's son, with all his fancy-schmancy degrees, has gotten tired of playing around out there in education, and is joining the company. Since blood is thicker than ability he will succeed his father, not me. I'm in no hurry, and my job isn't in jeopardy, but, someplace, somewhere, before I hang up my spikes, I'd like to be numero uno. If you hear of anything, put me in touch, as I'm interested in moving."

Again, the listeners open their mental file drawers and insert confidential information: "Presidency or potential presidency for good old Al." This kind of dynamic goes on constantly as these men socialize and relate, within their own country-club group and outside of it. They go about with their heads crammed full of confidential knowledge about job hunters and openings.

The men are actively involved in matching one to the other because they are all playing one-upmanship, trying to accumulate IOUs. If they can resolve one friend's problem through another friend, they have two people in their debt. Later they can collect favors in return or get repayment in kind if they are ever looking for a change themselves. This is how 80 percent of relocations take place and where the confidential information reposes. The next question is how to tap this reservoir, this resource, this underwater portion of the iceberg.

The first thing someone who wants to relocate has to do is to fill in the information gap, the communications void. Your country club friends may know all about you as a person. They are aware that you are a solid golfer, a dependable bowler, a tough man to bluff in a poker game, a man who doesn't psych while playing bridge, a great host, and a fun guy at a party. But they don't know anything about how you perform on the job. They may know where you work and your title, but they don't know what you've done.

Have you merely presided over an operation you inherited from someone, performing largely as a house-keeper? What impact have you had, and what input have you put into where you are or have been? Have you improved things, made changes for the better? Have you made money, saved money, solved problems? Will you be missed after you're gone? Will you have left your mark, your imprint, on where you've been? Or will no-body miss you or even remember you were there after you leave? What was your input, your contribution?

Remember that your friends don't know about such things because talking business is a no-no that everybody avoids when socializing. It is incumbent upon you as the seeker to give them the facts. You must relate them in a way they all can understand, regardless of their discipline. The approach cannot take the format of a technical job description. That would only make sense to people in the same technology or discipline as yours. Consequently, it would be too limited. Regardless of what they do, they all understand the bottom line, solving problems that stand in the way of greater profitability and making and saving money. You must communicate in common terms they can all understand. You must let them know your accomplishments in simple terms.

RÉSUMÉ

Put together a résumé. At the top of page one you center your name, address, and telephone number. Immediately below and to the left, state broadly the field you want to work in (never a specific job title), such as *Objective*: Sales/Marketing Management; *Objective*: Manufacturing/Engineering Management; *Objective*: Financial Management; or *Objective*: Administrative Management. This only takes one line.

Immediately below and to the left list *Accomplishments*. Under this heading, name problems you have encountered, what you did about them, and the happy results. This listing must be as truncated as possible. Strip out the adjectives and adverbs. Use only nouns and verbs. Do not show the details and techniques of what you did; just state broadly that you "revised" or whatever. The happy result must be finite, but not in dollars and cents. Use percentages instead.

Do not say your company was in an awful mess when you came aboard, but you straightened everything out, and now all is great. Such a blue-sky approach is meaningless. Being specific in terms of dollars can also be counterproductive. Some youngster fresh out of training might state, "In two years increased the volume from my sales territory from $20,000 to $60,000 a year." In the eyes of some viewers this accomplishment might seem minor, almost petty. Someone in manufacturing management might say, "Revised the process on the principal item in our product line, effecting annual production cost savings of $15 million." Such a statement might scare away a small company that has the perfect job for this man. It might be afraid that this heavyweight would pooh-pooh a small operation that doesn't even crank up

$15 million in total sales volume. It would fear that if it hired this man he'd very quickly get bored and unhappy and leave. The two never get matched up because the company has been frightened off beforehand.

The aspiring salesman would be better advised to say, "Trebled the volume from my sales territory in two years." The manufacturing manager should have said, "Revised the process on the principal item in our product line, effecting annual production cost savings of 15 percent." In both cases the viewer could translate the percentages in terms of his own reference framework. Neither man would strike out because he was considered underqualified or overqualified for a company's operation.

Do not enumerate your accomplishments by discipline or job on your résumé. In order not to overlook any plusses, thoroughly wring out a list of what you did at each place you've worked, and put each accomplishment on a 3 by 5 card. After you've finished your listing, select the two best and lead with these. Finish strongly with your third or fourth best accomplishments, including the remainder at random. By riffling your 3 by 5 cards as you would a deck of playing cards, you can come by a random mix.

If, for example, you've moved from engineering to production, don't list all your engineering accomplishments consecutively and follow with your production claims to fame. We can sustain reader interest better by interspersing the two. The reader might get bored by what you've done in engineering because it's irrelevant to his needs and stop reading. He has production problems but doesn't get that far down your list, and you've missed an opportunity. Try to hold each accomplishment to one sentence, two at the most. If you need more room perhaps you can break it down into two or more parts. The more accomplishments you can show, the better.

If you have many accomplishments, try to list them all without worrying about aesthetics like plenty of white space or double-spacing. If you are not looking for a creative job in the graphic arts, such niceties of layout and composition aren't important. Your track record, what you've done, is what counts. Show them, even at the risk of having two solidly typed pages. Of course, if you have fewer accomplishments, you can dress up the presentation with margin indentions, double-spacing, and lots of white space.

Either way, however, the résumé should never exceed two pages. It should never include job descriptions, delineation of duties, responsibilities, number of people you supervised, descriptions of products you're familiar with, or salaries. All these unnecessary data will make your résumé look like a business obituary, and will frequently have an excluding, counterproductive effect. Your résumé is intended to convey that you understand the name of the managerial game as well as your mission in management, which is to make money, save money, and solve the problems standing in the way of making and saving even more money. Stressing your accomplishments will demonstrate this awareness to any reader, regardless of discipline. Use of job description

---

data is too limiting. Such information will only be understood by, and be of use to, those few people who are your same breed of cat and in the same field.

The format of your résumé, then, should be as follows:

Earnest Hopeful
123 Main Street
Town, State, Zip
Phone (Area) 456-7890

OBJECTIVE: Production Management, Chemicals

ACCOMPLISHMENTS

Revised the process on the principal item in our product line, effecting annual production cost savings of 15 percent.

Changed material handling methodology, enabling 18 percent greater production while reducing up-front inventory of raw chemicals by 12 percent.

Devised simpler batch mixing and control, enabling same production volume with 15 percent reduction in line personnel.

Go on with the balance of your accomplishments.

WORK HISTORY

1966–1968	XYZ Corporation, New York—Management Trainee
1968–1970	ABC Corporation, New York—Staff Asst. to V.P. Production
1970–1974	ABC Corporation, Chicago—Asst. Plant Manager
1974–Present	LMNOP Corporation, Chicago—Plant Manager

Note that we have not mentioned salary.

EDUCATION
> BSCE, New York University 1966
> Currently MBA candidate, De Paul University, nights

MILITARY
> U.S. Air Force 1957–1961. Enlisted Private, discharged Captain.
> Graduate Officer Candidate School, School of Applied Tactics, Intelligence School, MOS 1014 Forward Air Controller.
> Two years overseas service Korea 1960–1961

AFFILIATIONS
> Professional Engineer, State of Illinois
> Member, American Chemical Engineering Society
> Chairman, Greens Committee Forest Park Country Club
> Vice President, Flyaway Skeet Club
> > *Show both professional and personal or social involvements, especially any office you held or other recognitions of your leadership by your peers.*

PERSONAL DATA
> Married: Two children, still at home, boy 14, girl 12
> Height: 6 ft   Weight: 180 lb   Health: Excellent
> Will travel and/or relocate   Age: 38

You may find that your résumé runs longer than the two-page maximum. One way to cut down on the verbiage is to work up from the bottom of page two, beginning with the givens that can't be cut. This will show you the precise amount of space left for the Accomplishments category.

GETTING AUDIENCE

Even the best résumé and the best cover letter ever put together by anyone anywhere will not get you a job. At best, they will merely get you a hearing. In order to be hired, you've got to be both salesman and product, simultaneously. Mass mailings all over the marketplace are ineffective, time consuming, and expensive. Few such mailings reach the right hands because they are incorrectly addressed to begin with, usually to presidents.

If such a letter ever survives all the people who pass it on, including a protective secretary, the president will probably junk it himself. He will reason that the sender is completely naive, sending the letter to him when it should have been addressed to someone a few rungs below him. Because he is turned off by the obvious ignorance of reality, that president is hardly likely to pass the letter down to the proper person. A petitioning letter should only be sent to a president if the position you are seeking is one in which you would report directly to him. If, in the usual course of things you would be reporting to someone below him, address your letter to that person: Mr. Harry Brown, Vice President of Production.

Researching the names of these people in hundreds of companies and addressing them personally can mean an awful lot of wasted time and postage. Most such recipients probably have a full staff, so the effort will be largely misdirected and little attention paid to your mail. (If it is the usual form of letter and résumé it probably won't be read at all.) In other words, we are completely off target as far as the 80 percent of the iceberg of job potential goes. Remember what we said earlier. These are the places we want to tap, and we have the means to do so — our accomplishments-oriented résumé.

We use the résumé as a ploy to get audience, and getting the audience is what we need in order to get situated. Audiences upgrade into interviews, and interviews into offers, especially now that you know how to display objectivity and how to handle yourself during interviews. Most importantly, we are bridging information gaps about ourselves as professionals, enabling ourselves to get matched up to a job. People who may know us well personally are now able to compare and consider us as possibilities for some of the unlisted, unpublished opportunities they have heard about in confidence.

Advice Calls

The way we use the accomplishments résumé is to phone our friends and say, "Ed, as you (probably) know, I'm at a crossroads in my career, and I'm trying to get it redirected the most intelligent way I know. Since I've had very little experience at marketing myself, I'm looking for advice. I've prepared a tentative résumé that I'm showing to several dozen friends like you — men whose experience and judgment I trust and value highly. I'm asking them for their advice and commentary. After I've made the rounds, I plan to distill out a consensus form of résumé that I'll go to press with. When can I have five or ten minutes of your time to go over the résumé with you and get your advice?"

You might narrow the options down a little more by saying "I'm going to be passing your building Tuesday morning and Thursday afternoon, so I could stop by either time. Which would be more convenient for you?" Your friend suggests 10 A.M. Tuesday or 2 P.M. Thursday. Maybe he'll invite you for lunch instead. At any rate, you'll get your five or ten minutes, more likely an hour or two, plus many free meals. Your friend probably won't refuse you. You've flattered him and set him up as an authority figure. You haven't endangered your association by coming to him hat in hand, begging for a job. If he doesn't have one, it can be an embarrassment for both of you.

Your pride is intact, and you're both safe as far as your relationship continuing in unspoiled fashion. You've only asked for advice, and advice is free. Most of us dearly like to give it. In fact, many of us overdo it, running around ramming unwelcome and unsolicited advice down a lot of gagging throats: "If I were you, I'd do this instead of that." You are not making a pain of yourself. Instead, you are an asset your friend may be able to utilize as he goes about playing his own games, picking up IOUs he can cash in later.

You meet your friend, bringing along your portfolio. Show him your résumé. As he reads it, you hope that it will ring a few bells for him. Now that he is learning for the first time what you do as a professional, he'll open his mental file drawers containing confidential job opportunities and start comparing and connecting you with them. He'll attempt to make a match.

It is unlikely that your friend will blue-pencil your résumé. He may make some commentary about the format being unusual, but he is going to be much more concerned with the content, with what he is learning about you. However, if he does suggest revisions, play the game with him. Make notes of what he thinks would be an improvement.

The résumé, of course, is not tentative. It is final, and not to be changed. If someone later asks how come you're using the same format when he had suggested changes for the better, you have an easy answer. Just tell him that you showed the résumé to thirty-five or forty people. Out of that group only four or five men besides him suggested changes. (Don't ever single him out by saying he was the only one who wanted to make revisions. Give him some company, whether he had it or not.) All the others told you not to change a word of it, so you went by the majority consensus and left it as is.

Instead of giving you a critique of your résumé, your friend is far more likely to give you names of people he thinks you should see. For example, he might think you are a possible replacement for Jim Jones, the minimally performing plant manager who is bugging his golf-playing buddy Joe. He can check your fit for this situation very easily. He calls Joe and says "Ed here, Joe. I have a friend at my desk who is looking for advice on a tentative résumé he's been showing me. Since I'm a lawyer, I'm not in too good a position to advise him. He's in your discipline, Joe, in chemicals manufacturing as a plant manager. Since you're both in the same business, I can't think

of anyone better qualified than you to give him the advice
he's looking for. Are you free for lunch today? If so, let's
the three of us meet."

Joe's ears are going to waggle when he hears chemicals plant manager. He knows his long-time foursome
member Ed heard his gripe at the nineteenth hole several
Saturdays back. He'll put two and two together and will
accept the luncheon invitation, even if he has to cancel a
previous appointment. He'll recognize the game that is
being played, and go along with it. He knows that Ed
isn't going to risk announcing that he's found a replacement for Joe's plant manager. There's the matter of compatibility to consider.

Had Ed taken the risk and sent you to Joe, he might
receive a phone call from Joe a little later to the effect that
Ed might be a real legal eagle but he knows nothing
about chemicals manufacturing, and that Jim Jones on his
worst lazy day is head and shoulders above the guy he
sent over to replace Jones. A fine relationship of many
years could become somewhat strained, if not endangered.

Instead, Ed is playing it safe. Without telling you that
this is a genuine opportunity for you, he is introducing
you on a first-name basis to a guy who needs someone
like you. You are getting the benefit of his sponsorship.
You will be treated by Joe as a peer, a friend of a friend,
not as a stranger. And, you will not be competing with
hundreds of others. This will be a simple one-on-one situation. You're either right for the job or you're not.

Ed hopes that Joe will have a chance to look you over

and to check out your objectivity during the conversation at lunch, and that Joe will say "Earnie, you don't need any advice on your résumé. I can use someone like you over at my operation. After lunch let's go back to my shop. I'll show you around and we can talk further." You're now a long way toward becoming part of that 80 percent placement statistic on confidential job openings. You'd have to behave pretty badly to blow it now. Knowing what you know from this book, you're hardly likely to do that.

The worst that can happen is that Joe doesn't like what he sees and hears. He may decide that you're too strong or too weak or that for some other reason you would not be compatible to him and his operation. But he is involved with you through your mutual friend Ed. He cannot throw in his cards and quit playing the game. He'll suggest other people to whom you can go for advice under his aegis. These will be people out of *his* confidential file drawers, people he believes you could be more compatible to, and vice versa.

If you're too strong for Joe and he figures the two of you would be constantly clashing, he may know of some weaker person who is looking for a powerful back-up man to pretty much call the shots. There is a refining process that goes on in these advice-call situations. By the second or third referral you should really be in the right ball park. A chain-letter effect takes place when advice calls are made. Like a stone dropped in a pond, referrals cause a rippling effect in all directions. The people to whom you go for advice or to whom you are referred are going to react as practical and pragmatic problem solvers in response to your approach. Only rarely will they come on like grammarians about your résumé. Instead, they'll give you names, in the hope they can become the catalyst, the instrument, for resolving two problems simultaneously, thereby ending up with two people in their debt.

During those infrequent instances when the person you are calling on for advice does not volunteer names, ask for them. He undoubtedly knows of opportunities, but he may be inexperienced at playing games. In fact, it may never have occurred to him. Get him started by asking. Don't come away empty from any advice call you make. You'd be breaking the chain-letter effect and you might soon run out of names, which you don't want to happen.

The author has kept statistics for years on thousands of advice calls made by hundreds of men. On the average, every ten advice calls made results in an offer. The usual number of advice calls made has been between thirty and forty, resulting in three or four offers from which to choose. There is no faster or better single way to get yourself situated or relocated in a career slot, rather than just another job to replace the one you lost or quit. If you took any old job, you could be going out of the frying pan into the fire.

You may say you've only been in your town a very short while and consequently know only a few persons on whom you could make advice calls. You don't have to know many people. One will do for openers. If that person gives you a couple of people to see and each of these give you a couple more, you'll be starting a pyramid.

In fact, you could be a complete stranger, knowing absolutely nobody in town, and still make advice calls. In that case start with the town bank or banks. There are more bankers on corporate boards than people in any other profession, including law and accountancy. Because they are approached for financing, they get advance intelligence about upcoming plans for expansion, renovation, removals, and additions. They know practically everybody and everything that's going on in town.

The top officers of most banks are rarely involved in operational matters. The day-to-day running of the bank is usually delegated to cashiers and assistant cashiers. The top men perform mostly as counselors and consultants. As part of their full service offer they make themselves accessible to the public. Therefore, they are available for advice calls. And they have even more than the usual amount of knowledge of the confidential opportunities that make up the 80 percent of the annual placement action. They'll see you. They'll do it on prospect, in the hope that you'll open your personal accounts with them or come to them for mortgage or other loans, or keep them in mind if and when you are in a position to swing company business their way.

You may get as many as a half-dozen names of some of the most important people in town, people who can use your talents, from a bank president or executive vice president. Phone them saying the banker suggested you

call (if he doesn't call for you) because of their high qualifications to give you advice on your tentative résumé.
Because a banker referred you, they will not dare to refuse to see you, of course, even though you are a stranger
and not even a long-time friend of a friend. As you go
through the same advice-call procedure you would with a
friend of one of your friends, the same gamesmanship dynamics set in. You'll get further referrals, a lot of audiences and exposure, and offers. You'll also get to know a
lot of influential people who can be of use to you later, if
not immediately.

In just a few weeks of advice calls you can get to see
and meet just about everybody in town who is important.
If you handle yourself objectively and demonstrate compatibility, if you have any kind of track record or potential, offers have to be forthcoming from this group of the
town's top people. And you'll no longer be unknown, a
stranger in a strange town.

Advice Letters

Obviously you can only make advice calls on people
who are close by geographically. You don't want to take
long-distance trips for this purpose unless there is a specific city you want to relocate in for some reason. If that
is the case and you can afford the time and expense, go
there for a couple of weeks of concentrated advice calls,
starting with the bankers if you don't know anyone else.
You should hit pay dirt as far as referrals are concerned.
If you know a lot of people scattered all over the country
and are open to relocation, you can utilize these contacts

by writing letters asking for advice on your résumé. The content of these letters should approximate your advice-call pitch, as follows:

Dear Tom:

As you may or may not have heard, the LMNOP plant that I've been managing in Chicago is being shut down in sixty days. There are no openings at other LMNOP plants around the country, so I'm at a crossroads in my career, and must move on.

Since I have never had to market myself before, I haven't had any experience that could be of help to me now. I've learned, however, that when a smart business-man is faced by a problem he is not competent to cope with, he gets expert consultative help. This is what I'm doing now.

Enclosed is a copy of a tentative résumé I've put to-gether. I'm sending these to three or four dozen men like you around the country, men whose judgments I respect and value highly. I'm asking these friends for advice and commentary on the résumé. After I've gotten back their replies I'm going to distill out a consensus form of résumé. I will then go to press with it and send it to a select list of companies.* By the way, that list is not yet complete, so if you have any suggestions, any names to add to it, I'll be glad to have those along with your résumé commentary.

I'm looking forward to your response.

Gratefully,
Earnie

*If you prefer to remain where you are, add "here in Chicago (or wherever), where I prefer to remain." If you want to relocate to some other specific spot, write, "send it to a select list of companies in the San Francisco area (or wherever)." The fact that the person you're writing to is in Boston doesn't mean he or she won't know of possibili-ties for you in Chicago or San Francisco.

It would be wrong to decide beforehand that somebody you know can't be of help because he is not that high on his business totem pole. He may come by considerable confidential knowledge of the 80 percent placement activity variety in his social life. Maybe porters don't hobnob and play golf with presidents, but a night porter can drop a résumé in the president's "in" basket while he's cleaning up his office. Be thorough and utilize your total resources.

A good place to start might be your Christmas-card mailing list. Include classmates, fraternity brothers, guys you were in service with, former co-workers and bosses, former competitors, former customers, former suppliers, former neighbors, former fellow church members, former anything. The only question you should ask is, was our relationship good enough and close enough while it lasted for him to take the time and trouble to respond, even though our orbits have been out of phase for some years now? If the answer is yes, send the advice letter.

The advice letter can either be handwritten or typed. If typed, however, add a handwritten postscript at the bottom to soften, to personalize, by referring to something out of your past relationship.

> *"P.S. When are you and Jane coming out for a visit?*
>
> or
>
> *P.S. How are Mary and the kids? The children must be getting big by now.*

or

P.S. Barbara sends her best.

or

P.S. Do you think we'll ever make it back to the Pub?

or

P.S. Did you ever break 100 again?

You'll get back replies saying yours is the most un-usual résumé they've ever seen, but don't change a word of it. It's now in the hands of the vice president of production, who will be in touch. Other responses will say, "I've sent it to the ABC Company and suggest you send two more to the DEFGH Company and the XYZ Company, to the attention of so and so, and let me know when you mail them so I can follow up for you." Still other replies will say, "Any friend of John Paul Jones is a friend of mine, and on paper you look great, so when you get this give me a jingle to set up a date for an interview."

This last letter may give you pause because you don't know a John Paul Jones. You have to remember your friends are not going to junk your résumé. They'll pass it along. The friend you originally wrote for advice may have given it to a friend or someone in his company. The point is, call for the appointment anyway, only mention-ing briefly that John Paul Jones is more of a friend of a friend than a friend of yours. The sponsorship, the peer introduction, is still there and working for you. You are not coming in cold, alone, and a total stranger. You've had a lot of icebreaking help.

Thank-You Notes

As you make advice calls and get replies to your advice letters be sure to follow Emily Post. Be courteous by sending thank-you notes. Don't use your wife's stationery. It may be pastel-colored, scallop-edged, or even scented, any and all of which would be inappropriate. Get yourself some plain white 6 by 9 notepaper with envelopes to match from your stationer. Handwrite, don't type, these notes.

> Dear Mr. James:
>
> Thank you for the time, courtesy, and advice you gave me on Tuesday, the 14th. I've been in touch with the two men whose names you gave me, and will be seeing Mr. Compton on Friday and Mr. Andrews on Monday.
>
> After I have gotten their advice, I will let you know the outcome.
>
> Gratefully,
> *Earnest Hopeful*

Keep these contacts alive, as they can be of use to you later. By your courteous follow-up you'll let them know you weren't using them and then forgetting them — ships passing in the night. Getting such notes may prompt them to rummage further through their minds for other places to send you. If they've learned of something new since you've last seen them, they'll be much more disposed to put you in touch. A recipient of such a note might even say, "This guy is not only great, he's courteous, and courtesy is in very short supply around here.

That project we've been holding back on will need a smooth guy like him to head it. Instead of keeping it on the back of the stove for another six months, we'll move it up to the front burner now, and bring him in before we lose him. I like the way he operates and how he handles things."

So, keep everybody you've asked for advice informed along the way as to what's happening. Be sure to let everyone know the final outcome, where you're going as what for whom. Try to stay in touch after you're situated by an occasional phone call, note, or luncheon. You might wind up getting offers later from people who aren't ready for you now. This courteous maintenance of contact may seem like too much bother. If that's the case, the second law of human nature is at work in you. Sublimate it. Don't let invaluable assets dry up and blow away through your neglect. Some of these people may even become customers or clients of yours, or a source of hard-to-get material for your new company.

There is no better or faster way to find a new career position than through advice calls and letters, utilizing your accomplishments résumé as an excuse. There is an additional benefit to be derived from this tactic. Top-level managers do not bother answering want ads, listing themselves with employment agencies, or visiting search firms. Instead, when they want to make a change, they drop fleas in the ears of their friends and their friends' friends in the fashion we've described. In other words, they make advice calls. They play the game. They utilize their friends and contacts in an acceptable and understood way, just as their friends would utilize them if the roles were reversed.

Even though you may never have been in top management, you're behaving and proceeding as a top manager would. You're demonstrating that you understand the relocating process, that you're aware of the realities. Consequently, you'll be viewed as a peer, as one of the boys with the smarts. You'll be credited with having top manager potential because you're acting like one, even though you've never yet been one. Your managerial image will be enhanced by the way you're going about solving your personal problem.

You will not be demeaning yourself and your image by going the less productive, lowlier, route taken by the great majority, those who don't know any better. They devote the bulk of their efforts to answering want ads, despite the Department of Labor's statistic that all the ads placed in all the newspapers and trade publications in the country account for only a tiny fraction of the placements made annually at $15,000 and above. To make matters worse, most people don't even know how to answer an ad!

Advice calls are best made from 9 to 5, Monday through Friday. During those hours you should arrange as much as possible to get audience with somebody. There is plenty of time left in the evenings or even on weekends to write advice letters and answer want ads. Even though want ads are the least productive means available to you, don't disregard them completely. You

218

don't really care where your career solution comes from. That isn't important. Be thorough. Answer want ads too.

Want Ads

The average unknowing man answering want ads assumes he is in some kind of contest for which in case of a tie, the earliest postmark wins. He lives in the suburbs somewhere, and early Sunday morning he drives to the railroad station newsstand to pick up his copy of the *New York Times* or the *Chicago Tribune*. He goes home and sequesters himself all day, writing a half-dozen or more ad responses. Late that night he drives back to the station to drop his letters in the mail so that they'll catch the 1:04 A.M. milk train into town. He wants his letters on somebody's desk first thing Monday morning. And he succeeds, along with hundreds of other guys.

It never occurs to any of them that the unknown executive they conjure up in their minds, and to whom they are addressing their life histories, is going to be too busy to wade through this huge stack of replies. That chore will be delegated to someone else, a clerk, stenographer, secretary, or somebody in personnel. Obviously, some criteria for retention or rejection are going to be established for that reader's guidance. Such criteria can be highly idiosyncratic, but three of the more commonly used are:

1. *Excessive Length.* Responses should not exceed two pages of cover letter and two pages of résumé.

2. *Salary History.* Replies should not include past

earnings, even though they were specifically asked for in our ad. Any guy naive enough to disclose this information to an unknown, a blind box number, is not for us.

(This is not so much an information-seeking question as it is an evaluative question regarding your business sophistication and awareness. For every time that you'll be disqualified for not having given salary information, you'll be disqualified ten times for having given it. Just think for a minute. If some stranger walked up to you on the street and asked you what kind of money you're making, would you tell him? You'd first want to establish some validity to justify such a disclosure. The same principle pertains here in answering want ads. If you're not the right, compatible man for the job, what difference does it make what you're willing to work for, down to and including, for nothing?)

3. *Excessive Use of the First Person Pronoun.* Scorekeep as you read — every time the word "I" appears at the start of a paragraph, give it three demerits. Every time "I" starts a sentence, give it two demerits. Anytime "I" appears anywhere in a sentence, give it one demerit. When you reach a total of twelve demerits, throw away the reply. That person will never be the team guy we're looking for. He'd be a loner — too subjective, self-centered, and self-concerned.

To get past screeners and unknown criteria, to reach Mr. Big's eyes only, delay your response by at least a week. Sunday is a great day to answer want ads — the ones that appeared in the *previous* Sunday's papers. By the time your response reaches Mr. Big the spate will have dwindled to a trickle. Yours might be the only reply he's received that day, so he'll have time to read it personally, which is what you want. You won't be too late. You'll be coming in at the right time from the point of view of Mr. Big's psychology. He'll be discouraged by all the faulty earlier replies and will be saying to himself, "Isn't there anybody out there who is what I'm looking for?" Your right-on-target response will reach him with maximum impact. At the very least, you'll be different from all the others, which alone is worth delaying your response for.

The average uninformed person who answers want ads doesn't know how to read them. He gives equal value to everything that appears in them, which is wrong. Every ad will have one or two "musts," and then maybe a half-dozen extras that it would be nice for you to have in addition. The equal-value replier doesn't have the musts but does have all the extras. He says to himself, "I can cover six of the eight things asked for. The other two I can learn or fake, so I'll respond." Of course, he's not qualified. Similarly, he has none of the half-dozen extras but is heavy on the two musts. He says to himself, "I've only got two of the eight covered, and six are too many to learn or fake." He doesn't respond, even though he is qualified.

Don't take some of the educational qualifications mentioned in the ads too literally. For example, the MBA bit is heavily overdone. Some recent graduate just starting in personnel may be writing ads from the job descriptions submitted him by managers. For want of work experience, he relates to and draws from what he knows best — academe. In his naiveté, he may think that some of the skills and knowledge called for by the job description could only be found in someone with an MBA, so he tacks this qualification on.

Also, you've got to keep in mind that everyone tries to get the best and the most for the money he spends. People start high in a bargaining situation in the expectation that they'll have to come down, discount, and settle for less than what they originally asked for. Every company would dearly like to have a 25-year-old PhD with thirty years experience who will work for $5,000 a year. Obviously, there ain't no such animal, but some of this impossible dreaming intrudes into many want ads. They overstate mostly in the matter of educational requirements. If you have the other musts but not the MBA or other advanced degree mentioned, reply anyway. If you can do the job, what difference does your formal education make? You could be a kindergarten dropout and be qualified!

There is something else you should know about want ads. The open ads showing a company's name are legitimate, but many of the blind box-number ads are not. Precise figures are not available. Some of the best-informed guesstimators believe that as high as 50 percent of these are not legitimate. The opening that is being described does not exist. The anonymity of blind box ads encourages them to be used as a resource for all sorts of ulterior purposes.

For example, a personnel manager somewhere has lost touch with what a certain kind of job is worth in the current market. He writes an ad, and hundreds of replies come back that include salary information, giving him his answer. (You want to avoid aiding, abetting, and encouraging such fishing expeditions. That is another reason not to include your salary history even when it is requested.)

Somewhere a boss may be getting tired of being bugged constantly for more money by a pushy subordinate. He writes an ad describing exactly what this guy does. Again, back come hundreds of replies. Some are from people who are better educated, less expensive, and more experienced than the incumbent. The boss clubs his subordinate on the head with these letters, and his demands subside. The ad mission has been accomplished. Only if the demands don't stop does the job opening become legitimate, but the subordinate isn't likely to continue pushing or to quit. He's seen the ad replies and knows he was being unrealistic and greedy. He knows there are better guys out there willing to work for less money. Finally and most importantly, he knows the boss has a long running start on finding a replacement for him. In fact, he realizes that the batch of replies contains some from candidates the boss would prefer to him, so he behaves.

A group may decide that the exotic product line it has put together doesn't lend itself well to the usual channels of distribution; it will have to be marketed by direct mail.

No appropriate mailing lists are available; their product line consists of ship's bells, capstans, bowsprits, and port and starboard running lights. They solve their problem by writing a big generic and fictitious ad aimed at any person who was ever in the Navy, Coast Guard, or Merchant Marine; who has ever been on water, fresh or salt; who has ever owned or rented a boat of any kind; who has ever been out on a party boat or charter boat; or who aspires to any of these things. They place these ads in a dozen major newspapers around the country, especially those near water, and back come thousands of responses. None of these respondents ever hears any more about the job, but in a couple of weeks each receives a four-color brochure describing nautical products, with purchases resulting.

To get back to answering ads: The average person gives too much information. He spills not only his work history, but his life history, for page after page. He tips his hand. He leaves all his fight in the gym. There's nothing left to talk about at the interview. He's told so much he's inviting the recipient to make an immediate decision. Since that person cannot make an affirmative decision without seeing the man, the decision that is made is negative. Lastly, his response may be rejected by the initial screener because of excessive length, and Mr. Big may never get to see it.

The average uninformed person who answers want ads does so in a negative, self-disqualifying fashion. He writes, "I'm a little short here, I'm a little light there, I'm not quite what you want here, I have only five years instead of ten years there. Somehow, in spite of all this, you may think I'm qualified. With a lot of luck, and if I make a novena for the next nine days, I may hear from you." Such negativism is highly communicable. The recipient will probably agree that the man is not qualified if the response hasn't already been knocked out of the race through the demerit system because of excessive use of the first person pronoun "I."

The way to answer a want ad is as follows: Make the decision as to whether you're qualified. Don't leave it to them. If you have the musts, you are. Give just a one-page response. Don't include education, age, salary, or work history, and never send a résumé. Merely play back to them the wording of their ad, saying, "Yes I am."

For example, the ad might state, "We're looking for a 10-foot-tall, 500-lb guy with blue hair and curly teeth who can swing a left-handed monkey wrench while whistling 'Dixie.' " Don't say that you're only 9 feet 6 inches but still growing; that you weigh only 450 but if you go on a crash banana diet you can make 500 in only a few weeks; that your hair isn't blue, it's only lavender, but it is getting darker all the time; and that your teeth are only crinkly, not curly, but your orthodontist can fix that up. What you're telling them is that you're not qualified, that you aren't what they're looking for, and that you shouldn't even have bothered responding. If you are qualified, tell them so as positively and briefly as possible, playing back their own terminology:

Box 1234
Chicago Tribune

Gentlemen:

In response to your ad of Sunday, September 23, I am a ten-foot-tall, 500-pound guy with blue hair and curly teeth who can swing a left-handed monkey wrench while whistling "Dixie," and for encores I can whistle "Coming Through the Rye."

When can we get together?

Sincerely,
Earnest Hopeful

This unaccompanied-by-anything one-page letter reaches Mr. Big's desk and his eyes more than a week after his ad appeared. It is probably the only positive letter he received. It is not too long, it does not contain salary information, it does not contain an excessive use of the pronoun "I," and it says you are what they are looking for in their own words. Mr. Big will be motivated to pick up the phone and find out more about you. This is what you want — to find out who they are so you can start making an early judgment as to whether you want to work for them or not if you get as far as an offer.

When Mr. Big (or anybody else) calls, don't let yourself be interviewed in depth on the phone. When he asks "Where did you do this?" you reply, "With the ABC Company from 1967 to 1969. When can we get together?" He may persist with "Where did you pick up so and so experience?" You respond, "With the XYZ Company from 1970 to 1974. I'm available for an interview tomorrow morning or Thursday afternoon. Which would be better for you?"

The phone is a better means of communication than the mails in that it permits flexibility, vocal inflection, meaningful pauses, and embellishment or revision of opportunity, none of which is possible in a letter or exchange of letters. However, our objective is not to get telephone interviews; it is to get face-to-face interviews so you can utilize the techniques you've been learning in order to get offers. Keep your phone answers as short as possible without being rude or crude, and keep asking for an in-person audience, just as a salesman keeps asking for an order.

A salesman does not go through his pitch, then stare the prospect straight in the eye and ask, "Well, are you going to buy or not?" That would put the prospect under pressure. He would have to take a big, deep breath and say yes or no. A good salesman would use a low-key approach and gain an affirmative decision by way of minor points. Order pad out, he would say, "Which color do you prefer, the pink or the blue?" "I like the blue." "When would it be more convenient for you to take delivery, the first or the fifteenth of next month?" "The fifteenth." "Do you want six gross or twelve gross?" "Why don't we try eight gross?" "Okay, will you write your name here at the bottom?"

Use this same technique when you are contacted on the phone by the people who placed the ads you've answered. Don't let it become a question of whether they will see you or not. Proceed positively in the expectation that they will see you, the only question being *when*. Steer and control here by offering a couple of times as options for them to choose from. Instead of pink or blue ask which would be better, Tuesday morning or Thursday afternoon. Have them make a choice, not a decision.

To recapitulate on how to answer a want ad: Wait at least a week before replying. You make the decision that you're qualified, not them. If you have the "musts" required to do the job, respond. Do not be deterred by a lot of superfluous window dressing that may appear in the ad. Write a single-page response, playing back their wordage and telling them, "Yes I am." Do not mention salary, age, education, or where you've worked before. Do not enclose a résumé. Do not use or include any other kind of form or "canned" approach. Each ad should be given individualized, custom-tailored treatment, based on its wording. You'll get more responses than you've ever had before. Lastly, don't get interviewed over the phone. Tell them no more than you have to to get audience, and give them a couple of optional times for your meeting, letting them choose the most convenient.

Motivating Letters

Now you know how to make advice calls, how to write advice letters, how to handle thank-you notes, and how to answer want ads. There is one last thing you can do if you have to, although the previous three penetrations into the marketplace should be enough. Make up a list of twenty or thirty *local* companies you'd like to work for because of their fine reputation, great product line, growth, or dynamics. Be sure these local companies can use somebody with your skills. If you're exclusively a kumquat-dicer, do not include on your list a firm that only makes widgets. It couldn't use you, and you'd be wasting everyone's time. Look these companies up in any of the various directories available at your library or at your present place of employment. Find out the name of the man heading up the function you'd be part of, and address a letter to him:

> Earnest Hopeful
> Address
> Phone

Mr. John Brown
Vice President, Production
AEIOU Chemicals Company
123 Main Street
Town, State, Zip

Dear Mr. Brown:

   If you are having problems in your production management, perhaps help is at hand. During my years in chemicals production management, many accomplishments have accrued to my credit. Listed below are a typical few:

   Revised the process on the principal item in our product line, effecting annual production cost savings of 15 percent.

   [Follow with your best accomplishments as shown on your résumé, filling no more than one page. Leave room at the bottom for the following short close.]

   Having done such things before, it will be even easier to do them again—perhaps for you? Please expect a phone call from me in about a week to check that possibility.

> Sincerely,
> *Earnest Hopeful*

The purpose of this motivating letter to Mr. Brown is to describe some problems you've solved that his incumbent staff hasn't yet. He may be at full staff, but you haven't asked for any specific position as manager of something or other. If you did, Mr. Brown might say "I've already got one of those," and read no further. Whether he is at full staff or not, you can be sure he has problems. Hence our approach as a chemicals manage-*ment* problem solver, not as a chemicals plant manage*er*.

Hopefully, some of your accomplishments are going to hit him where he is hurting for answers. If you push his "on" button only once, he may say to himself that his staff is pretty far down the road toward a solution, and he won't be especially motivated to see you. If you touch a couple of sore spots, you've got a good chance. Hit him where he's hurting in three or four places, and he probably won't wait for your phone call. He'll call you instead. If compatibility checks out okay, he'll bring you in and cap you down on the incumbent staff. He'll create a job for you; he wants his problems solved so that he may make a greater profit faster. The money you'll be saving and making for him should be much greater than what you'll cost. The title of the job he creates for you isn't important. It could be as his assistant or as his roving, trouble-shooting ambassador, with or without portfolio. It could be as head honcho.

If you don't hear from him first, phone him in a week as promised, and shoot for an audience. He may stall by saying that he's not ready for you yet but will keep your letter on file and will be in touch in about six months to see if you're still available. Don't buy this. Remember your mission, which is to get face-to-face exposure. Tell him that as an objective manager you know that compatibility is the hiring key. Real estate is costly and there is no point in his cluttering his files with paper on people who may not fit. You're going to be passing his office a couple of times this week, Tuesday morning and Thursday afternoon. Which would be more convenient for him to spend ten or fifteen minutes with you checking out your chemical reactions to each other? If compatibility turns out to be good, you'll leave a more comprehensive résumé for his files and later use.

By getting audience you may be able to get him to advance his timetable rather than lose you. He can't reasonably expect you to wait six months and still be available. Even if he can't move his schedule up to make room for you and has no current need for you, you can turn the interview into a modified advice call. This time you're not just asking for advice, you're looking for a job. Ask him if he knows anyone who might be able to use someone like you.

Try to salvage something from this meeting opportunity. Try to convert this negative into some kind of positive step toward your career advancement. Keep getting audience, keep selling your product (you) by displaying it. Even an inept salesman will make sales if he displays his product often enough. By the law of percentages he's going to encounter some people who need his product and will buy it, take it from him, in spite of a poor presentation.

ALLOWING ENOUGH TIME

Be careful to dribble out your motivating letters. They are not to be mass mailed. The author's statistics show that you can expect an audience to result 50 percent of the time. If you can only make room for one interview a week, send out two letters a week. If you have time for two meetings, send out four letters. In this way you can manage and control your time and availability.

If you mail too many motivating letters at a time and start getting a 50 percent response for audience as you make your follow-up calls, you're going to have problems of your own creation to face. You'll have to guess, to make subjective judgments, as to which ones to see and which ones to skip because you certainly can't see them all. This guessing game will not be conducive to your career happiness. Later you'll be wondering and worrying about your selections, and whether you would have been better off exploring some of the other opportunities rather than the ones you did explore. You may have lucked into taking the very best situation available for you out of the whole bunch, but you'll never know, because you never got a chance to compare them all.

Be thorough, anticipate, and trickle out the letters no faster than you can keep up with appointments. Availability doesn't mean thirty minutes out of your lunch hour. Be prepared to spend a minimum of a couple of hours each time you get an audience; it will be more akin to an interview than to an advice call. Advice calls usually go faster because they are made on friends who already know a lot about you and friends of friends who accept you because you are sponsored. You can assume some time control over advice calls. If you're running late and are due back somewhere or are due somewhere else, you can break off and resume another time.

In interview situations you have no control over time; you go along as required, letting the interviewer do the terminating. The same applies to a motivating letter audience; you are not seeking advice from a friend or a friend of a friend. You're looking for a job from a stranger. It will take longer. Budget enough time so that you won't be obviously nervous about being late getting back to work or wherever. You certainly don't want to break off an audience, especially if things are going well for you. Leaving might turn off the interviewer. You might not be invited back to pick up where you left off because your conduct was viewed as unbusinesslike, unprofessional, unprepared, unanticipatory, and unobjective.

Since you are in no position to exert control, you've got to place yourself at your interviewer's disposal regarding time. Be sure that you've allowed enough time so you won't have to hurry or crowd matters. A leisurely interview is hard enough both ways, and you need to decompress any pressure. This can't be done if you are introducing a new pressure like time constraint, something that shouldn't be part of the picture at all. Just as your interviewer is making time for you, you've got to make time for him. Better to give yourself too much time than too little.

You may be thinking of making a change, but you

don't want to jeopardize your job in the meantime because you've got obligations and responsibilities. You pretty much have to account for your time or you're chained to your desk, with no opportunity or excuse to be out on the street. You've got a problem to resolve. Even if you make advice calls on your friends on your lunch hours or after 5 over a drink at some bar there are limits to how much you can presume.

The friends of your friends, the second or third referrals, will be less likely to want to meet you at odd times. They're doing you a favor by seeing you to give advice, even though they expect to derive some future benefit from it. They'll expect you to accommodate to their convenience. Similarly, the people whose names you get in response to your advice letters are going to expect to see you between 9 and 5, Mondays through Fridays. Interviews and quasi-interviews resulting from your motivating letters are not going to be held evenings or weekends. The same pertains to companies you hear from in response to your want-ad answers. And what about out-of-town interviews?

Before you start marketing yourself you may have to condition your boss or bosses to your being away now and then. Maybe you'll have to play sick. Maybe you can manage some fiction about extensive dental work or ongoing therapy of some kind that will involve leaving at noon a couple of days a week for a month or two. Maybe you can take your vacation in half-days or days. If worst comes to worst, get your campaign so organized in advance that you can shift it into high gear during the two or three weeks of your vacation. By the time your vacation is over you should be so far down the track, so confident and encouraged, that you'll be able to resign without fear, knowing you'll be relocated shortly after your separation. Keep in mind that you can only hide things for so long; sooner or later your boss will have to learn you're in the process of leaving. You're not going to walk out cold on him; that's no way to get a good reference. In fact, you could spend the rest of your working life trying to live down this kind of blot on your track record.

Unless you are that rare bird who does not have to account for his time, who is free to come and go as he pleases, time will always be a problem to some degree, the degree depending on your work circumstances. No pat, all-purpose solution exists for this problem; no two people are in an identical situation. Each individual will have to work it out in accord with his own circumstances.

As a manager or an aspiring manager, you are supposed to be able to solve problems. If you have a time problem, work it out. You'll find answers if you look hard enough. No book can tell you what to do. The factors involved are so myriad, differ so much in degree, and exist in such a variety of combinations of age, education, and experience, that we could hypothesize forever and still not cover your particular situation. Only you can do something about it. Just as nobody can go out on an interview or advice calls for you, or even go with you, there are other things you've got to do for yourself.

The last resort and worst solution to a time problem

is to squirrel away every penny you can until you have a cushion, a reserve that will carry you for a few months. Then quit, and get moving fast on your marketing program with your time competely freed up and your conscience completely clear. It is better to become unemployed than to be fearful and nervous, though employed, as you look for something better. An on-and-off, hot-and-cold, now-and-then approach might cause you to spoil a lot of relocation potentials. You might not find anything better because you could not conduct your campaign properly or adequately. You may also jeopardize your present position. Leading such an unsuccessful "double life" would certainly also frazzle your nerves.

If none of the suggested options, including this one of last resort, is acceptable to you, maybe you'd better stay put and forget about trying to accelerate your upward mobility. Your ambitions would be unrealistic and not at all in keeping with your limited abilities. You'd be showing that not only you can't solve problems, but that you can't make decisions. If you can't do for yourself, how can you expect to do things for somebody else as his surrogate or manager?

With a postal-clerk complex, you should dig in where you are and devote all your attention to what is obviously your greatest need, maintaining your security. To be a meaningful manager, not just a ribbon clerk or a housekeeper, requires courage. If you don't have it, or it's in short supply, you wouldn't be compatible or competent in a managerial role. In that case, for everyone's sake, especially your own, forget about enhancing your career through job changes. Your present employers recognize your weakness but, luckily for you, tolerate it and put up with it. Somebody else somewhere else might not, and you could quite possibly have a very hard time of it anywhere except in civil service.

Before you make a move to move, try to analyze and evaluate yourself, dig for some honest insights. If you don't have the intestinal fortitude that management requires, don't aspire to it. You would be operating in a world of fantasy and delusion. If you have the guts, go, man, go. You now have the know-how to do it successfully.

FINALE

There is no magic or mystery in marketing yourself. There are many ways to do it. Some are better than others. The methods outlined in this book may not be the best, but there are no better ways available that are widely known or in common usage.

Many of the points made were already familiar to you. Others may have been less well known. We've tried to wrap all the bits and pieces into one ball, to put it all together. Most readers can accomplish or attain everything suggested here. There is nothing esoteric in the marketing methodology outlined. It is all plain common sense, horse sense. If applied, it will assist you in achieving your career goals, assuming they are realistic. And if you are a dreamer of impossible dreams, what you've read may help to bring you down to earth, to reality.

At any rate, you know what it's all about and what to do about it. Your excuses are gone. This awareness and knowledge will give you a tremendous advantage over most of your peers and many of your superiors—the great majority of people who out of ignorance proceed in a highly subjective fashion.

Good luck with your marketing campaign. Using the precepts you've learned should give you the desired successful result. Once you've gotten your career started or restarted, remember to continue to behave objectively on the job and not to revert to your former subjectivity. If you revert, you will not be performing as advertised, you won't be delivering the goods, and your career may be a short one. Try to live the rest of your life by, and with, the lessons in this book.

May that life be long, happy, and successful.